B A C H
The Passions
Book I : 1723–25

BY

CHARLES SANFORD TERRY

Litt.D. (Cantab.), Hon. Mus.D. (Edin.)
Hon. D.Litt. (Dunelm.), Hon. LL.D. (Glasg.)

GREENWOOD PRESS, PUBLISHERS
WESTPORT, CONNECTICUT

Originally published in 1926
by Oxford University Press, London

First Greenwood Reprinting 1970

Library of Congress Catalogue Card Number 75-109864

SBN 8371-4355-1

Printed in the United States of America

Prefatory Note

THIS volume and its sequel exceed the require-
ments of those whose interest in Bach's Passions is
confined to the two that survive. I preferred to treat
the subject exhaustively, because there is no other
book on the subject, in English or foreign literature,
accessible to the student, whose needs this Series
serves. Lack of space prevents me from tracing the
development of Passion music to Bach's epoch. For
that preliminary chapter I refer the reader to my
article in the new (3rd) edition of Grove.

The analyses of the St. John and St. Matthew
Passions intentionally are non-technical. Their principal aim is to stimulate the listener's interest by
revealing the intimate relationship between Bach's
music and his libretti. The *Leitmotif* was as much
his characteristic as it was Wagner's a century later.

New translations of the texts of the St. John and
St. Matthew Passions are provided; those in English
use being unreliable and misleading. These are
metrically true to the originals and do not violate
Bach's declamation. In the Recitatives especially, but
not exclusively, English editors have taken liberties
with Bach's text which are the less excusable because
they are gratuitous.

Book I, in addition to an Introduction outlining

I   A 2

4 *Prefatory Note*

the conditions under which Bach produced his Passions at Leipzig, deals with the St. John Passion and Picander's text written in 1725. Book II, besides a short Conclusion, treats the St. Matthew and St. Mark Passions and discusses the St. Luke Passion in relation to Bach's asserted authorship.

Many will welcome the information that Miniature Scores of the St. Matthew and St. John Passions are published respectively by Eulenburg and the Vienna Philharmonischer Verlag.

C. S. T.

KING'S COLLEGE,
OLD ABERDEEN, *September* 1925.

CONTENTS

BOOK I

Introductory

THE earliest catalogue of Bach's compositions, compiled in 1754, four years after his death, enumerated among his unprinted works ' Fünf Passionen, worunter eine zweychörige befindlich ist '.[1] Half a century later, Forkel repeated (1802) a statement which for him had authority.[2] The number tallies, moreover, with the five sets of Church Cantatas attributed to Bach. His Masses also number five. The Scores of two Passions are extant. Some of the music of a third (1731) survives in the *Trauer-Ode*. Christian Friedrich Henrici, who wrote under the pseudonym ' Picander ', published a Passion libretto in 1725 which Bach may have set to music. There is extant also the Score of a St. Luke Passion which Spitta deemed authentic, and the Bachgesellschaft published as genuine in 1898. Thus, the ' Fünf Passionen ' are as follows :

1. The St. John Passion, 1723.
2. Picander's Passion, 1725.
3. The St. Matthew Passion, 1729.
4. The St. Mark Passion, 1731.
5. The St. Luke Passion, *n.d.*

Before examining these five works it will be helpful to explore the conditions under which they were performed. Bach, as Cantor, was responsible for the

---

[1] The so-called ' Nekrolog ', reprinted in the *Bach-Jahrbuch*, 1920.

[2] *Johann Sebastian Bach* (ed. Terry, 1920), p. 138.

music in five Leipzig churches, in only two of which,
however—St. Thomas's and St. Nicholas's—Passions
such as he composed were sung under his direction.
Uninterrupted by the Reformation, the Passion Story
had been sung in Holy Week at Leipzig since the
fifteenth century, a plainsong Recit. with simple
faux bourdon chorus passages.[1] The continuity of the
tradition was not broken until 1721, two years before
Bach's appointment. On Good Friday in that year,
we learn from the Note-book of Johann Christoph
Rost, Custos of St. Thomas's,[2] the Passion was sung
for the first time to concerted music in the Oratorio
style. Bach's predecessor, Johann Kuhnau's St. Mark
Passion was performed on this significant occasion,
and St. Thomas's, whose facilities were superior,
initiated the innovation. Rost indicates that it was
not repeated until 1723, when Bach's St. John Passion
was sung in the same church. St. Nicholas's first heard
the new Passion in 1724. Thereafter it was sung on
Good Friday at Vespers in the two churches alternately. Bach's appointment to the Leipzig Cantorate
therefore coincided with the new Passion's arrival
there. The ceremonial of its performance we learn
from Rost. On Good Friday afternoon at 1.15 the
church bells were rung. At 1.45 the service began
with the ancient Passion hymn, ' Da Jesus an dem
Kreuze stund '. Part I of the Passion followed, and
after it the hymn ' O Lamm Gottes unschuldig ',
whose melody Bach inserted into the opening Chorus
of the St. Matthew Passion. The sermon followed,
preceded by the Pulpit hymn ' Herr Jesu Christ,

---

[1] Two in Leipzig use are printed in Gottfried Vopelius's *Neu
Leipziger Gesangbuch* (1682).

[2] The manuscript is among the archives of St. Thomas's, to
whose authorities I am indebted for facilities for transcribing it.

dich zu uns wend '.[1]   Part II of the Passion was then
performed, and, after it, Gallus's Motett 'Ecce
quomodo moritur justus '.[2]   The Passion Collect was
then intoned :

Deus qui pro nobis Filium tuum crucis patibulum subire
voluisti, ut inimici a nobis expelleres potestatem, concede nobis
famulis tuis ut per ejusdem Filii tui passionem a morte perpetua
liberemur, per eundem Dominum nostrum Jesum Christum.
Amen.[3]

Rinkart's hymn, ' Nun danket alle Gott ', was then
sung, and the long service concluded with the Blessing.

All of Bach's Passions were first heard at St.
Thomas's,[4] at a service of the character described above.
It is possible to visualize the surroundings.   The performers were placed in the organ gallery at the west
end of the nave.[5]   The larger of the church's two
organs stood against the west wall at the back of the
gallery, and, when Bach came to Leipzig, had been
there for two centuries.   It had been renovated in
1721, and under Bach's supervision was entirely
reconstructed in 1747.[6]   The smaller organ, which
originally stood beside it, was taken out of the gallery
in 1639 to a position opposite, on the south side of
the tower separating the nave from the chancel.   It
was removed from the church altogether in 1740.
Rost particularly notes that in 1736 both organs

[1] For the tunes and English translations of these hymns see
the present writer's *Bach's Chorals*, Pt. III (1921).
[2] In Vopelius (p. 263) ; for four parts (C. A. T. B.).
[3] For the Leipzig liturgy see the present writer's *Joh. Seb.
Bach : Cantata Texts sacred and secular* (1926).
[4] Rost shows that the Passion was sung at St. Thomas's in
1723, 1725, 1729, 1731.
[5] Illustrations of the interior of St. Thomas's are in the work
referred to in note 3.
[6] Spitta, ii. 281, gives the specifications of the two organs.

were used for the Passion performance. The gallery
also contained a Clavier; among the parts of the
St. Matthew Passion is a 'Continuo pro Cembalo'
for Coro II, written throughout and figured in Bach's
hand. Grouped right and left were the singers and
instrumentalists: their numbers are discussed in
connexion with the St. Matthew Passion, which made
larger demands than others upon Bach's resources. A
recent writer [1] supposes the Evangelist to have sung
from the lectern between the nave and the chancel,
an untenable suggestion. Bach's singers and a small
orchestra of Strings, Flutes, Oboes, and Fagotti
were massed under his close observation in the
gallery. The organ was played by St. Thomas's
organist: if both were used, probably St. Nicholas's
organist officiated at the smaller. Bach's place was
at the Cembalo, where he could keep the performance
together, beating time when necessary.[2] From the
gallery the performers looked down upon the congregation in the nave facing eastward, women in the
centre, men on either hand. In the aisles of the
nave, north and south, the galleries faced inwards.
A low screen divided the chancel from the nave, in
the middle of which rose the lectern, from which the
Collect and Epistle were intoned on other occasions.
The pulpit stood against a pillar on the south side of
the nave.

[1] Wilhelm Werker, *Die Matthäus-Passion* (1923).
[2] A woodcut dated 1710 shows Kuhnau in the front of the
gallery beating time with a scroll in his right hand. It is worth
pointing out that Bach endeavoured to shift the Passion performance from St. Nicholas's to St. Thomas's in 1724, partly on
the ground that the Clavier in the former church was out of
order (Leipzig Council *Acta*, 3 April 1724).

I. *The St. John Passion*
(1723)

APPOINTED to the Cantorate of St. Thomas's on 22 April 1723, Bach was formally inducted on 31 May, having on the previous day (First Sunday after Trinity) conducted his first Cantata at the morning service. The Cantorate had been vacant nearly a year [1]; but Bach's appointment was probable, if not assured, since January 1723, when Christoph Graupner withdrew reluctantly from the field. These facts bear upon the production of the St. John Passion. Certainly it was composed at Cöthen during the winter of 1722–3; for Bach was a candidate for Kuhnau's post early in December, if not in November 1722, and, if appointed, could expect to be in office before Good Friday, 1723, when Passion music would be required. In fact the appointment was not made until Good Friday had passed. Spitta therefore concluded that the St. John Passion was first heard on 7 April 1724. Much more probably it was produced in 1723, a bare fortnight before Bach's official appointment was made. For the Council hardly can have omitted to arrange for the repetition in 1723 of a commemoration so recently inaugurated. The assumption is supported: in 1729, on a vacancy occurring in the New Church, the Council arranged for one of the candidates to provide Good Friday

[1] Johann Kuhnau died 5 June 1722.

music. It is therefore reasonably certain that Bach's
earliest Passion was sung in St. Thomas's on Good
Friday, 1723.

The provision of a libretto caused Bach anxiety.
Not yet in touch with those at Leipzig who helped
him later; long since removed from his Weimar
literary collaborators; and having been for some years
released from writing Church music, he appears either
to have constructed his libretto himself or to have relied
upon some one as little expert. His choice of St. John's
text is difficult to explain except upon the assumption that he was directed specifically to set it. For
its narrative of the Passion, beginning abruptly with
Judas's treachery, omits striking episodes—the Institution of the Holy Supper, Christ's Agony in the
Garden, the earthquake, and the rending of the
Temple Veil. To interpolate them all was imprac-
ticable; but Bach borrowed from St. Matthew's text
the account of the earthquake and of Peter's remorse.

The libretto consists of St. John's chapters xviii
and xix, with the additions from St. Matthew's
Gospel already noted; fourteen congregational hymn
stanzas; and twelve original lyrical pieces—the first
and last Choruses, eight Arias, and two Arioso movements. All but three of the twelve are borrowed,
without acknowledgement, the majority of them from
the popular *Der gemarterte und sterbende Jesus*, written
by the Hamburg Councillor, Barthold Hinrich Brockes,
in 1712, a Passion text which Bach, alone almost
among contemporary musicians, did not put to music
in its entirety. His acquaintance with it dated at
least from 1720, when he visited Hamburg. He may
then have seen Handel's setting of it, the Score of
which exists partly in Bach's hand. Engaged in 1722
on an urgent and unfamiliar task, it was natural to

seek the assistance of a libretto famous throughout Germany. Its influence can be traced in eight of the twelve lyrical pieces of the St. John Passion.

No. 1 (Chorus). Excepting the first two lines, which are borrowed from Psalm viii. 9, the words appear to be original, and may be attributed to Bach or his librettist. The movement was first used in 1727.

No. 11 (Aria). With minor alterations, the text is borrowed from Brockes's opening stanza :

Brockes, 1712	Bach, 1723
Mich vom Stricke meiner Sünden	Von den Stricken meiner Sünden
Zu entbinden	Mich zu entbinden,
Wird mein Gott gebunden.	Wird mein Heil gebunden.
Von der Laster Eiterbeulen	Mich von allen Lasterbeulen
Mich zu heilen	Völlig zu heilen,
Lässt er sich verwunden.	Lässt er sich verwunden.

The alterations are slight and judicious, and the stanza very appropriately follows Caiaphas's ' It is expedient that one man die for the people '.

No. 13 (Aria). The words are original, and may be attributed to Bach or his librettist. An earlier version failed to satisfy the composer. Its variations are shown in italic type :

Ich folge dir gleichfalls { *mein Heiland, mit Freuden,* / mit freudigen Schritten, }
Und lasse dich nicht,
Mein Leben, mein Licht.
{ *Mein sehnlicher* / Beförd're den } Lauf
{ *Hört eher* / Und höre } nicht auf,
{ *Bis dass du mich lehrest geduldig zu leiden.* / Selbst an mir zu ziehen, zu schieben, zu bitten. }

No. 19 (Aria). The words are by Christian Weise (1642-1708), Rector of the Gymnasium, Zittau, a popular hymn-writer. The stanza is the first of five, entitled 'Der weinende Petrus', printed in his *Der grünenden Jugend nothwendige Gedancken* (Leipzig, 1690, p. 352). Bach's, or his librettist's, emendations are indicated in italic type :

Ach, mein Sinn,

Wo $\begin{Bmatrix} \textit{willst} \\ \text{denckst} \end{Bmatrix}$ du $\begin{Bmatrix} \textit{endlich} \\ \text{weiter} \end{Bmatrix}$ hin ?

Wo soll ich mich erquicken ?

Bleib' ich hier ?

Oder wünsch' ich mir

Berg und Hügel auf den Rücken ?

$\begin{Bmatrix} \textit{Bei der Welt ist gar kein} \\ \text{Ausser find ich keinen} \end{Bmatrix}$ Rath,

Und im Herzen

$\begin{Bmatrix} \textit{Stehn} \\ \text{Sind} \end{Bmatrix}$ die Schmerzen

Meiner Missethat,

$\begin{Bmatrix} \textit{Weil} \\ \text{Dass} \end{Bmatrix}$ der Knecht $\begin{Bmatrix} \textit{den Herrn} \\ \text{den Herren ganz} \end{Bmatrix}$ verleugnet hat.

The Aria was written for the 1727 performance. Presumably Bach found the words at Leipzig, where Weise's hymns had considerable vogue.

No. 31 (Arioso). The movement first appeared in the 1727 version. The words are derived from Brockes's text :

Brockes, 1712	Bach, 1727
Drum, Seele, schau mit ängstlichem Vergnügen,	Betrachte, meine Seel', mit ängstlichem Vergnügen,
Mit bittrer Lust, und mit beklemmtem Herzen,	Mit bittern Lasten hart beklemmt von Herzen,
Dein Himmelreich in seinen Schmerzen !	Dein höchstes Gut in Jesu Schmerzen,
Wie dir auf Dornen, die ihn stechen,	Wie dir auf Dornen, so ihn stechen,
Des Himmels Schlüsselblumen blühn.	Die Himmelsschlüsselblume blüht ;
Du kannst der Freuden Frucht von seiner Wermuth brechen !	Du kannst viel süsse Frucht von seiner Wermuth brechen,
Schau' wie die Mörder ihm auf seinem Rücken pflügen !	Drum sieh' ohn' Unterlass auf ihn.

As in the case of No. 13, Bach's text reached its final shape only after revision. The earlier version reads :

> Betrachte, meine Seel', mit ängstlichem Vergnügen,
> Mit bittrer Lust und halb beklemmtem Herzen,
> Dein höchstes Gut in Jesu Schmerzen.
> Sieh hier auf Ruthen, die ihn drängen,
> Für deine Schuld den Isop blühn,
> Und Jesu Blut auf dich zur Reinigung versprengen.
> Drum sieh ohn' Unterlass auf ihn.

No. 32 (Aria). The words are an improvement of Brockes's text :

Brockes, 1712	Bach
Dem Himmel gleicht sein bunt-gestriemter Rücken,	Erwäge, wie sein blutgefärbter Rücken
Den Regenbögen ohne Zahl als lauter Gnadenzeichen schmücken,	In allen Stücken Dem Himmel gleiche geht !
Der (da die Sündflut unsrer Schuld verseiget)	Daran, nachdem die Wasser-wogen
Der holden Liebe Sonnenstrahl	Von unsrer Sündfluth sich ver-zogen,
In seines Blutes Wolken zeiget.	Der allerschönste Regenbogen Als Gottes Gnadenzeichen steht.

The movement was first introduced in 1727, and the words (in the final Score) superseded a discarded stanza :

> Mein Jesu, ach ! dein schmerzhaft bitter Leiden
> Bringt tausend Freuden,
> Es tilgt der Sünden Noth.
> Ich sehe zwar mit vielen Schrecken
> Den heil'gen Leib mit Blute decken,
> Doch muss mir dies auch Lust erwecken,
> Es macht mich frei von Höll' und Tod.

The lines appear to be an expansion of Brockes's :

> Seh' ich, so oft man auf ihn schlägt,
> So oft mit Strick und Stahl die Schergen auf ihn dringen,
> Aus jedem Tropfen Blut der Liebe Funken springen.

No. 48 (Aria and Chorus). The text is adapted from Brockes :

Brockes, 1712	Bach, 1723
Eilt, ihr angefochten Seelen,	Eilt, ihr angefocht'nen Seelen,
Geht aus Achsaphs Mörder-	Geht aus euren Marterhöhlen,
höhlen,	Eilt — (*Chor.*) Wohin ? —
Kommt — Wohin ? — nach	Nach Golgotha !
Golgotha !	Nehmet an des Glaubens Flügel,
Nehmt des Glaubens Tauben-	Flieht — (*Chor.*) Wohin ? —
flügel,	Zum Kreuzes Hügel,
Fliegt — Wohin ? — Zum	Eure Wohlfahrt blüht allda.
Schädelhügel,	
Eure Wohlfahrt blühet da.	

Brockes's stanza, written for the ' Daughter of Zion and Chorus of Believers ', whose form Bach follows here, was copied by Picander later in the St. Matthew Passion (No. 70).

No. 58 (Aria). The text is original, and may be attributed to Bach or his librettist.

No. 60 (Aria and Choral). From the fourth line the text is borrowed from Brockes. Bach makes the Saviour's answer direct :

Brockes, 1712	Bach, 1723
Sind meiner Seelen tiefe Wun-	Bin ich vom Sterben frei-
den	gemacht ?
Durch deine Wunden nun	Kann ich durch deine Pein
verbunden ?	und Sterben
Kann ich durch deine Qual	Das Himmelreich ererben ?
und Sterben	Ist aller Welt Erlösung da ?
Nunmehr das Paradies erer-	Du kannst vor Schmerzen zwar
ben ?	nichts sagen,
Ist aller Welt Erlösung nah ?	Doch neigest du das Haupt

Dies sind der Tochter Zions Und sprichst stillschweigend :
Fragen :   Ja!
Weil Jesus nun nichts kann
vor Schmerzen sagen,
So neiget er sein Haupt und
winket : Ja !

No. 62 (Arioso). The text follows an idea
suggested by Brockes :

Brockes, 1712	Bach, 1723
Bei Jesus Tod und Leiden leidet	Mein Herz ! indem die ganze Welt
Des Himmels Kreis, die ganze Welt ;	Bei Jesu Leiden gleichfalls leidet,
Der Mond, der sich in Trauer kleidet,	Die Sonne sich in Trauer kleidet,
Giebt Zeugniss, dass sein Schöpfer fällt.	Der Vorhang reisst, der Fels zerfällt,
Es scheint, als lösch in Jesus Blut	Die Erde bebt, die Gräber spalten,
Das Feuer der Sonnen Strahl und Glut ;	Weil sie den Schöpfer sehn erkalten :
Man spaltet ihm die Brust — die kalten Felsen spalten,	Was willt du deines Ortes thun ?
Zum Zeichen dass auch sie den Schöpfer sehn erkalten.	
Was thust denn du, mein Herz ?	

No. 63 (Aria). Like the preceding Arioso, Bach's
text treats Brockes very freely :

Brockes, 1712	Bach, 1723
Was thust denn du, mein Herz ?	Zerfliesse, mein Herze, in Fluthen der Zähren
Ersticke, Gott zu Ehren,	Dem Höchsten zu Ehren.
In einer Sündfluth bittrer Zähren.	Erzähle der Welt und dem Himmel die Noth,
	Dein Jesus ist todt.

1   B

No. 67 (Chorus). Bach's libretto shows a marked superiority over Brockes's :

Brockes, 1712	Bach
Wisch' ab der Thränen scharfe Lauge,	Ruht wohl, ihr heiligen Gebeine, Die ich nun weiter nicht beweine ;
Steh', sel'ge Seele, nun in Ruh' !	
Sein ausgesperrter Arm und sein geschlossen Auge	Ruht wohl, und bringt auch mich zur Ruh'.
Sperrt dir den Himmel auf, und schliesst die Hölle zu.	Das Grab, so euch bestimmet ist, Und ferner keine Noth umschliesst, Macht mir den Himmel auf, und schliesst die Hölle zu.

Bach's text, as it appears in the Score, is the revision of an earlier preference :

> Ruht wohl, ihr heiligen Gebeine,
> Um die ich nicht mehr trostlos weine,
> Ruht wohl, ich weiss, einst giebt der Tod mir Ruh'.
> Nicht stets umschliesset mich die Gruft,
> Einst wenn mich Gott, mein Erlöser, ruft,
> Dann eil' auch ich verklärt dem Himmel Gottes zu.

Thus only three of the twelve lyrics (Nos. 1, 13, 58) are original. The fact points to the composer's perplexity over his libretto, an impression confirmed by the revision of the text to which attention has been drawn, and also by its unskilful construction. The two Parts are very unevenly balanced, and the distribution of lyrical pieces is not judiciously made. In Part I two of its three Arias (Nos. 11, 13) are separated by only three bars of Recitative. Nor is the text of No. 13 happily chosen. It comes after ' Simon Peter followed after Jesus '. But since the narrative of Peter's cowardice is told immediately, the words

So eager I follow and joyfully hasten

are unhappily chosen. A similar uneven distribution of lyrical numbers is observed in Part II. Two of the eight it contains (Nos. 58, 60) are separated only by two bars of Recitative.

Dissatisfaction with his libretto rather than his music must account for Bach's sacrifice of movements in the original version of the Passion when it had its second performance in 1727. They are five in number:

1. The Choral Chorus, 'O Mensch, bewein' dein' Sünde gross ', subsequently No. 35 of the St. Matthew Passion, replaced by No. 1 of the final Score.

2. A Bass Aria with Soprano Choral,[1] 'Himmel reisse, Welt erbebe ', which followed No. 15. The latter so adequately filled the situation that Bach withdrew the Bass Aria as redundant.

3. A Tenor Aria,[2] ' Zerschmettert mich, ihr Felsen und ihr Hügel ', which took the place of the present No. 19. Bach appears to have rejected it for the incongruity of its text, which seems to have been inspired by one of Salomo Franck's stanzas : [3]

Franck	Bach
Ihr Felsen, reisst ! ihr Berge, fallt !	Zerschmettert mich, ihr Felsen und ihr Hügel,
Ihr Klüfte gebt mir Aufenthalt !	Wirf, Himmel, deinen Strahl auf
Wie kann ich doch entgehen,	mich !
O Jesu, deiner starken Hand ?	Wie freventlich, wie sündlich, wie vermessen,
Zög ich gleich über Meer und Land	Hab' ich, O Jesu, dein vergessen !
Und über Berg und Höhen,	Ja, nähm' ich gleich der Morgenröthe Flügel,
Führ ich gleich in den Abgrund ein,	So holte mich mein strenger Richter wieder ;
Du würdest doch zugegen sein.	Ach, fallt vor ihm in bittern Thränen nieder!

[1] Printed in *B. G.* xii (1), p. 135.   [2] *Ibid.*, p. 142.
[3] The suggestion is Spitta's (German edition, ii. 350).

4. A Tenor Aria,[1] ' Ach, windet euch nicht so ', which was replaced by Nos. 31 and 32. Here, again, Bach's criticism evidently was directed upon the libretto, though the superiority of the text that replaced it is not evident.

5. The concluding Choral Chorus, ' Christe, du Lamm Gottes ', which was transferred by Bach to a similar position in the Quinquagesima Cantata, ' Du wahrer Gott und Davids Sohn ' (1724).

The Score and Parts of the St. John Passion are in the Preuss. Staatsbibliothek, Berlin. The Score (P. 28) bears the inscription: *J̃[esu] J̃[uva]. Passio secūdū Joānē à 4 Voci 2 Oboe 2 Violini Viola è Cont. di J. S. Bach.* Part II has not a separate inscription. At the foot of fol. 27 is the legend : ' Fine della Parte prima '. The following Choral (No. 21) is headed ' Parte seconda '. The manuscript contains 92 pages, of which only the first twenty are autograph, i. e. Nos. 1–13 and 14 to the entry of the Evangelist at bar 42. The pagination throughout is in Bach's hand, as well as the inscription on the last page, ' Fine D. J. C. C. Gl.' (' To our Lord Jesus Christ be all the glory.') The Score evidences Bach's careful revision. Written subsequent to the latest of the extant Parts, it represents the composer's final wishes in regard to the work. The Parts (St. 111) fall into three groups. The oldest set, of which the figured Organ part is lost, contains only two parts entirely autograph (Viola da Gamba and Tenor ' Servus '). Considerable portions of all the Parts, orchestral and vocal, are in Bach's hand, however, and the group represents the original 1723 version. Though the composer made considerable alterations for the second performance in 1727, the original Parts were not

[1] *B. G.* xii (1), p. 148.

entirely replaced ; for the new opening Chorus (No. 1
of the Score) is stitched up with them, while the new
Arias are similarly attached to the original Continuo
part. The Parts show considerable alterations subsequent to 1727. At one performance a Sinfonia
was substituted for Nos. 61–3 ; it is lost. The final
performance was marked by a return to the 1727
version.[1]

The Passion is scored for Strings, 2 Flutes, 2 Oboes,
Organ, and Continuo.[2] This orchestra invariably
doubles the voices in the Chorals, and accompanies
most of the Choruses. In Nos. 42, 44, 46, 54, all but
the last of which represent the Jews' expostulations to
Pilate, the second Oboe is an Oboe d'amore, a third
lower than the ordinary Oboe, and with a pear-shaped
bell, which fell into disuse after Bach's death. In
Nos. 62 and 63 Bach uses two Oboe da caccia or
hunting Oboes (Cor anglais). In No. 31 he introduces a Lute ; in Nos. 31 and 32 two Viole d'amore (a
sweet-toned instrument with 5–7 gut strings on the
finger-board and 7–14 wire strings underneath) ; in
No. 58 a Viola da gamba (corresponding to the
modern Violoncello, but lacking sonority). The
Recitatives throughout are accompanied by ' Organ
and Continuo ', the figuring (absent in the Score)
being derived from a copy of the Score made by
Hering, a chorister under C. P. Emanuel Bach at
Hamburg.

The characters are : Jesus (Bass), Maid (Soprano),
Evangelist (Tenor), Servant (Tenor), Peter (Bass),
Pilate (Bass). The Aria and Arioso movements are
distributed among the four voices.

---

[1] Cf. Rust's Preface to *B. G.* xii (1), and Spitta's note in vol. ii.
709.

[2] The Parts include ' Continuo pro Bassono grosso ' ; ' Continuo pro Cembalo ' ; and ' Continuo ', i. e. the Bass Strings.

PART I

I. PROLOGUE[1]

No. 1 (Chorus) (*Strings, 2 Fl., 2 Ob., Cont., and Organ*) :

> Lord, our Creator, Thou whose fame
> Is known of all men glorious,
> Now show us through Thy Passion's smart
> That truly Thou Eternal art,
> God's Only Son,
> Who e'en affliction did'st not shun,
> Yet reign'st victorious.

Unlike the opening Chorus of the St. Matthew Passion, there is no note of lamentation here, no bewailing of an imminent tragedy. Christ hangs upon the Cross crucified but triumphant. Over a persisting pedal, which never ceases except at three significant intervals, the Violins give out a subject, tranquil yet positive, a cloud of majesty over the Lord of heaven:

Ex. 1.
Vn. i, ii.
Va.
Vcelli.
& Fagotti.

[1] The sectional headings adopted here are not in the original text.

Above, the Flutes and Oboes wail out a theme of woe:

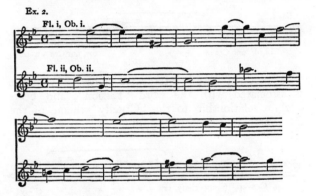

the significance of whose dissonances is revealed in No. 36:

Thus the first 32 bars expound two words—
'Creator', 'Passion'—Heaven, Calvary.   Calvary
recedes to the background as in rolling periods the
voices acclaim the Almighty.   At bar 33 the colours
change.   The tranquil semiquavers pass to the Continuo from the Strings : Flutes and Oboes continue
their threnody : while the voices, still upon the
words 'Lord, our Creator', declaim a fugal theme of
sinister connotation.   The vocal Basses introduce it :

Ex. 4.

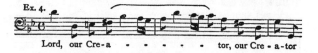

Lord, our Cre-a - - - - - tor, our Cre - a-tor

The sinuous phrase is interpreted at bar 58, where it
is associated with the word 'Passion', and bears
a close relationship to the 'Crucify' theme of the
St. Matthew Passion (No. 59) :

Ex. 5.

Cru-ci - fy, cru-ci-fy, cru - - - - - ci - fy!

Thus, the interpretation of the second section of
the Chorus (bars 33–9) is clear.   The voices acclaim
the Master of the universe, but in a phrase that speaks
of Calvary, which the Flutes and Oboes emphasize.
The section rests for foundation—significantly marked
by Bach himself *Tutti unisoni*—upon the original
subject of the Violins (Ex. 1), the theme of Godhead.
At bar 58 the fugal subject is definitely associated
with the Passion.   But as the movement proceeds the
tragic theme of the Flutes and Oboes (Ex. 2), though

persisting, is obscured; that of the Strings (Ex. 1) swells with increasing vehemence, the voices singing triumphantly, 'Yet reign'st victorious', in passages marked by Bach *forte*, till the Chorus ends upon an assertive crotchet. 'Death is swallowed up in victory.'

II. THE BETRAYAL

Nos. 2–6 (Recits. and Choruses) :
St. John xviii. 1–8 (The Betrayal).

No. 7 (Choral) (*Strings, 2 Fl., 2 Ob., con voci ; Cont. and Organ*) :

O wondrous love that knows nor stint nor measure,
Which nailed Thee to the Cross, O martyred Treasure !
I live on still, the world's delights enjoying ;
But Thou hang'st dying.

No. 8 (Recit.) :
St. John xviii. 9–11 (Peter and Malchus).

No. 9 (Choral) (*as No. 7*) : [1]
Thy will be done, O Lord, below
On earth, as 'tis in heaven also.
When sorrows round about us lour
O make us own and know Thy power.
Our stubborn flesh bend to Thy will
And with Thy grace our spirits fill.

---

[1] Though the same orchestra is employed for the Chorals throughout, excepting No. 60, the instruments do not uniformly double the same vocal part.

Bach's Recitative speaks a language spontaneous and natural, unfolding the narrative with the inflexions of a good reader, restrained but conscious of its dramatic force and poignancy. Throughout the St. John Passion it is impersonal except in the passages which describe Peter's weeping (No. 18) and the scourging of Jesus (No. 30). Elsewhere the Evangelist recites the story impassively at a mean pitch somewhat lower than in the St. Matthew Passion. The words of Christ are not, as there, marked by a distinguishing accompaniment. But His Recitative is of a dignified serenity which lifts His personality above the other characters.

The Evangelist's 'Whom seek ye ? ' (Nos. 2, 4) is answered in brief Choruses (Nos. 3, 5). In structure the two are one. But the second is pitched lower than the first ; as though a sense of awe followed the first tumultuous intrusion on the Saviour, an interpretation supported by Bach's orchestral treatment of the two. He embroiders both with a significant theme :

Ex. 6.

which appears again in Nos. 25, 29, 46, where, as here, His enemies seek the Saviour's life. Pitched high above the voices, it incites the mob with vicious darts of malice. In No. 3, played by the first Violins and Flutes in unison, it is particularly malevolent. In No. 5 it is heard a fifth lower, the Flutes are silent, and the subject is given to the first Violins alone.

Here must be pointed out a characteristic of the St. John Passion—it contains three Choruses (Nos. 23,

34, 38) that are duplicated; and one (Nos. 3 and 5) that is triplicated. Bach had no compunction in adapting his music to other words than those for which it was originally composed. But, excepting the B minor Mass, the St. John Passion affords the only instance of his doing so in the same work. Nos. 3 and 5 are repeated in Nos. 29 and 46; No. 23 in No. 25; No. 34 in No. 50; No. 38 in No. 42. Pirro [1] conjectures that by repetition Bach designed to represent the mood of the populace, unvarying in its obstinate rancour. Spitta [2] supposes that his unemotional libretto denied the composer opportunity for dramatic differentiation. Neither explanation is satisfactory; it is impossible to believe that Bach would have repeated himself to such an extent had he not written in haste and under the pressure of circumstances.

No. 7 is the first of the Chorals that punctuate the work, commentaries of the Christian faithful in the language of popular melody. The stanza is the seventh of Johann Heermann's 'Herzliebster Jesu, was hast du verbrochen' (1630), set to Johann Crüger's melody (1640). In the St. Matthew Passion also the first Choral is a stanza of the same hymn to the same melody.

The awkward incidence of No. 8, whose opening sentence belongs to No. 6, is worth notice only as an indication of the librettist's inexperience. The introduction of a second Choral (No. 9) so soon after No. 7 can be attributed to the same cause, or to Bach's consciousness of the libretto's weakness in reflective pieces. In the St. Matthew Passion, Peter's impetuous action does not call, as here, for a Choral.

---

[1] *J. S. Bach*, p. 183.
[2] *Op. cit.* ii. 524.

The melody of No. 9 dates from 1539, when it first appeared in association with Luther's version of the Lord's Prayer (1539), of which the words are the fourth stanza.

III. BEFORE CAIAPHAS

No. 10 (Recit.) :
St. John xviii. 12–14 (Christ is led before Annas).

No. 11 (Aria : Alto) (2 *Oboes, Cont., and Organ*) :
For my erring, my misdoing,
Is He now suffering,
Bound with thongs, sore goaded.
That He whole and pure may make me,
From death may free me,
Is He grievous wounded.

No. 12 (Recit.) :
St. John xviii. 15 (Peter follows).

No. 13 (Aria : Soprano) (2 *Fl., Cont., and Organ*) :
So eager I follow
And joyfully hasten ;
I'll ne'er leave Thy sight,
My Life and my Light.
O let me not stray,
But draw me to Thee,
Thyself standing near me
To guide me, to beckon.

No. 14 (Recit.) :
St. John xviii. 15–23 (Christ before Caiaphas).

No. 15 (Choral) (*as No.* 7) :

Who dares now thus to smite Thee,
And falsely here indict Thee,
My Saviour and my Lord ?
Thou knowest no transgression
As we, who make confession,
With marks of sin are deeply scored.

'Tis I and my misdoing,
As ocean's billows flowing,
Unnumbered as the sand,
'Tis I that have Thee wounded,
To judgement have Thee hounded,
And 'gainst Thee guiltless raised my hand.

In Brockes's text the words of the Aria (No. 11) are the opening Chorus ('Chor der gläubigen Seelen'). Handel treated them so. Bach sees in the Saviour bound an invitation to intimate personal grief, and chooses as his medium the voice through which invariably he preferred to express it. The orchestral colour is sombre, and the themes of the Oboes and Continuo, the former syncopated, the latter straining upward with effort, seem to portray the Saviour bound and stumbling in pain :

Ex. 7.

With maladroitness, after a short Recit. (No. 12),

Bach introduces a second Aria for Soprano (No. 13) to words incongruous in their context. The tripping semiquavers suggest in their regularity the happy

Ex. 8.

So ea - ger I fol - low And joy - ful - ly ha - sten;

pursuit of a beloved object in sight, and may be contrasted with the spasmodic rushes of the Daughter of Zion in the St. Matthew Passion (No. 36). The Flute obbligato shines out like a star guiding the believer to his goal. The words are confident and fit ill with the action of Peter, whom they represent.

The buffeting of Jesus (No. 14) is appropriately followed by stanzas iii and iv of Paul Gerhardt's 'O Welt, sieh' hier dein Leben' (1647), a hymn whose third stanza Bach uses in the same context in the St. Matthew Passion (No. 46). Here and there the melody is Heinrich Isaak's (?) 'O Welt, ich muss dich lassen', a tune of secular origin first printed in 1539. In the first version of the Passion, as has been pointed out already, a Bass Aria with Soprano Choral followed at this point.

IV. PETER'S DENIAL

Nos. 16–18 (Recits. and Chorus) :

St. John xviii. 24–7 ; St. Matthew xxvi. 75 (Peter denies Christ).

No. 19 (Aria : Tenor) (*Strings, Cont., and Organ*) :

Ah, sad mind,
Where can'st thou comfort find,
Where solace shall I seek thee ?
Must I stay
Or hence take my way,
Hills and valleys leave behind me ?
Ne'er this world can ease afford ;
For sin's guerdon
Is my burden,
Woe for me hath stored,
I the servant who denied his Lord.

No. 20 (Choral) (*as No.* 7) :

Peter, thoughtless, Christ denies,
E'en his God forswearing.
Jesus on him turns His eyes ;
Peter's tears are flowing.
Jesu, bend Thy gaze on me
When by sin I'm taken ;
Stir my conscience right to see
How I've Thee forsaken.

The Chorus, ' Art thou not one of His disciples ? '
(No. 17), makes vivid the eager interrogation of the
bystanders. It is the only Chorus in the work whose
tempo Bach indicates (*Allegro*), and the upward thrust
of the phrase declares the eagerness of the questioners:

Ex. 9.

Art thou not   one of   His   di - sci - ples?

The words ' Art thou not ' are repeated forty-six
times, now an inquiry, now a menace. In the Soprano
part Bach lays repeated emphasis on the word ' not ',

and in bars 8–9 particularly the question is peremptory.
The Flutes, Oboes, and Strings are *con S.A.T.*, adding
a tone of insistence to their clamour.

When he borrowed the words, 'And Peter remembered the word of Jesus' (No. 18), Bach failed to
recollect that St. John does not record it. Though
the melisma on the words 'and wept bitterly' is
much more exaggerated here than in the St. Matthew
Passion, and is supported by a chromatic progression
in the Continuo which expresses mental torture, the
effect is not so poignant. Another detail of realism
occurs in bar 8 to represent the crowing of the cock :

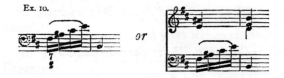

Ex. 10.

Bach followed tradition in this convention. Heinrich
Schütz, for instance, in his St. Matthew Passion
(1661) writes :

Ex. 11.

Und als - bald   krä   het der Hahn

As in the St. Matthew Passion, the Gospel verse
that records Peter's despair is followed by an Aria to
express his emotion. Here (No. 19) as there Bach
scores it for Organ and Strings. It lacks the Violin
Solo of the St. Matthew Aria, however ; though the
first Violin part is marked *Tutti gli Stromenti*, indicating
the composer's wish that it should be prominent. It

seems to represent the remorseful soul distractedly
searching for comfort :

Ex. 12.

The concluding Choral (No. 20) is the tenth stanza
of Paul Stockmann's 'Jesu Leiden, Pein und Tod'
(1633), set to the melody by Melchior Vulpius (1609).
Other stanzas of the hymn are used in Nos. 56 and 60,
and another in the abandoned Aria that followed
No. 15. Stockmann's hymn thus holds the place of
Gerhardt's 'O Haupt voll Blut' in the St. Matthew
Passion.

PART II

V. CHRIST BEFORE PILATE

No. 21 (Choral) (*as No. 7*) :

> *Christ, Who brought us to the light,*
> *Hath no wrong conceivèd,*
> *Yet was for our sins at night*
> *As a thief committed.*
> *Judged was He by wicked spite,*
> *Falsely some accusing ;*
> *Others, as the Book doth write,*
> *Buffet Him and wound Him.*

I   C

Nos. 22–6 (Recits. and Choruses) :

St. John xviii. 28–36 (Christ before Pilate).

No. 27 (Choral) (*as No. 7*) :

> *O Lord Almighty, wondrous is the story !*
> *How can my tongue enough exalt Thy glory ?*
> *What gift of price is there for man to give Thee*
> *E'er to repay Thee ?*
>
> *The mind of man its debt can never measure,*
> *Nor plumb the depth of God's eternal treasure.*
> *How ever can I by my feeble doing*
> *My love be showing ?*

Nos. 28–30 (Recits. and Chorus) :

St. John xviii. 37–end (Barabbas is preferred) ; xix. 1 (Christ is scourged).

No. 31 (Arioso : Bass) (2 *Viole d'amore, Lute, Cont., and Organ*) :

Consider, O my soul, with deep and anxious searching,
With heavy care weighed down thy heart within thee,
That Jesu's wounds release will give thee.
For, from the thorns that grievous pierce Him
Will heavenly blooms of blessing spring.
There shall the sweetest fruits rise from the gall they
        give Him ;
So, look with constancy on Him.

No. 32 (Aria : Tenor) (2 *Viole d'amore, Cont., and Organ*) :

> Take comfort !
> Know, His body torn and bleeding
> Will, hence proceeding,
> Soon heavenward wing its flight.

Take heart !
O'er sins like waters surging,
O'er billows of thine ill deeds' urging,
God's rainbow bright of grace is glowing
To show thee pardoned in His sight.

Nos. 33–9 (Recits. and Choruses) :

St. John xix. 2–12 (Pilate seeks to release Jesus).

No. 40 (Choral) (*as No. 7*) :

Thy bonds, O God's Almighty Son,
To grace on high will lead us.
Thy prison is a royal throne
Whence Thou in love dost speed us.
For hadst Thou not known bondage sore
We had been slaves for evermore.

The Choral (No. 21) which so appropriately begins
Part II is the first stanza of Michael Weisse's ' Christus,
der uns selig macht ' (1531), set to an adaptation (1531)
of the ancient ' Patris sapientia, veritas divina '.

The Saviour's trial before Pilate is rendered intensely
vivid by the short dramatic Choruses in which, with
extraordinary force, Bach expresses the malignity of
the Jews. Pilate's question, ' What accusation bring
ye ? ' unlooses their pent-up hatred on the snarling
phrase (No. 23) :

At bar 15 a new rhythm enters, vengeful in its hammer-like insistence, whose significance is fully revealed in Nos. 36 and 47 :

It is a vivid picture of the mob fanatical, insistent, implacable, and, as in No. 17, the normal orchestra supports the voices. The second Chorus (No. 25) answers Pilate's ' Then take ye Him and judge Him '. The theme of snarling menace (Ex. 13) is repeated, and with it (on the Flutes and first Violins in unison) the darting theme of vindictive hate (Ex. 6) already heard in Nos. 3 and 5. Excepting the Flutes and first Violins, the instruments (Vn. ii, Viola, 2 Oboes, and Cont.) are *con voci*.

No. 26 contains an unusual melisma, the single occasion where the Saviour betrays emotion :

The Choral (No. 27) is on the eighth and ninth stanzas of Heermann's hymn already heard (to the same melody) in No. 7.

Vainly Pilate seeks (No. 28) to release Jesus under the Passover custom of amnesty. In a short Chorus (No. 29) of four bars, the Jews with deliberate uniformity reject Christ and ask for Barabbas.   Both

Flutes, with the first Oboe and first Violins in unison, play the theme (Ex. 6) already heard so often, busy tongues of malice lashing the mob to anger. The other instruments are *con voci*. Pilate yields, and in a remarkable passage the Evangelist describes the Scourging. In the Continuo Bach represents the falling blows by the rhythm he employs in the St. Matthew Passion (No. 60), and which Handel associates with the words ' He gave His back to the smiters ' in the *Messiah* :

The Evangelist uses a prolonged and exaggerated melisma on the word ' scourged '. At first it matches the rhythm of the Continuo, but breaks from it, as though the torturer, impatient of restraint, had lost his self-control.

The Bass Arioso (No. 31) was not in the original Score. It has its counterpart in No. 74 of the St. Matthew Passion ; over both of them is an atmosphere of twilight stillness and calm produced by their orchestral setting. For one of the performances of the St. John Passion Bach substituted the Clavier for the Lute, an instrument of waning vogue in his period. A Part also exists with the direction, in his autograph, ' Wird auf der Orgel mit 8 und 4 Fus Gedackt gespielet '.

The Tenor Aria (No. 32) that follows brings us again to the tortured Saviour. The rhythmic figure of scourging pervades it ; but in the arching curves of the melodic lines we seem to see, as Schweitzer comments,[1] the rainbow of forgiveness of which the stanza speaks :

[1] *J. S. Bach*, ii. 181.

Ex. 16. Va. d'am. i.

The dramatic Chorus (No. 34), 'Hail, all hail', is full of the pictorial touches in which Bach delighted. In mocking homage one vocal part after the other (with the Strings supporting) enters upon the phrase:

Ex. 17.

Hail, all hail now, migh-ty King of Jew - ry!

while the Flutes and Oboes (which alone have independent parts), in rapid descending semiquavers, obtrusively make a ribald gesture of obeisance:

Ex. 18.

Notice also the exaggerated motions of the Continuo:

Ex. 19.

In a similar manner Bach represents the homage of the Sages to the Infant Jesus in the *Orgelbüchlein* :

Clothed in purple and crowned with thorns, the Saviour faces the mocking crowd and hears its angry shout (No. 36), ' Crucify, crucify ! ' From one side comes the dissonant howl already heard in No. 1 (Ex. 2). From the rest, with feverish reiteration and to a relentless but natural rhythm, comes the imperative demand :

Throughout the two themes are interwoven. Passion grows to frenzy and culminates in the sustained shout of the Basses at bar 22 :

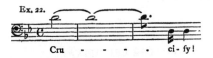

Throughout the Flutes and Oboes double the S.A.T.

In marked contrast stands the next Chorus (No. 38). Pilate has protested, ' I find no fault in Him ' (No. 37).

The Jews, lately clamouring tumultuously, now in deliberate counterpoint demand their Victim :

It will be noticed that in the third bar of Ex. 23 Bach significantly associates with the word ' perish ' (*sterben*) the figure (cf. bar 61 of No. 1) of the Crucifixion :

The orchestra is normal and *con voci.*

A Choral (No. 40) brings the Scene, so full of incident, to an end. The stanza is from Christian Friedrich Postel's Passion (*c.* 1704). The melody is Johann Hermann Schein's ' Machs mit mir, Gott, nach deiner Güt ' (1628).

VI. THE CRUCIFIXION

Nos. 41–7 (Recits. and Choruses) :

St. John xix. 12–17 (Jesus is led to Golgotha).

No. 48 (Aria (Bass) and Chorus) (*Strings, Cont., and Organ*) :

Haste, ye mortals sin-beladen,
Seek ye here your sorrows' haven!
Haste!

        Chor.   But where?
To Golgotha!
Poised on wings of faith so trusty,
Fly!

        Chor.   But where?
To yonder Calvary;
For salvation waits you there.

Nos. 49–51 (Recits. and Chorus) :

St. John xix. 18–22 (The Crucifixion).

No. 52 (Choral) (*as No. 7*) :

> *Within my deepest being*
> *Thy Name and Cross always*
> *Shine bright and glow unceasing,*
> *To yield me joy and praise.*
> *O ever shall it stay me*
> *And comfort my last breath,*
> *That on the Cross of Glory*
> *Thou once did'st hang in death.*

Nos. 53–5 (Recits. and Chorus) :

St. John xix. 23–7 (Jesus commends His mother to John).

No. 56 (Choral) (*as No. 7*) :

> *Still He planned for others' good*
> *As He hung there dying ;*
> *To His mother, where she stood,*
> *Comfort, love, supplying.*

O my soul, the lesson learn ;
Love thy God and neighbour.
So thy soul will He not spurn,
But give life for ever.

The Jews renew their insistent demand (No. 42),
' If thou let this man go thou are not Caesar's friend.'
Their chant is pitched a semitone lower than in No. 38,
the incongruity of whose music to these words is
patent. The phrase which assumed such significance
associated with the word ' perish ' is here sung to
the word ' Friend ' (Freund) ! As in No. 38, the
orchestra (normal) is *con voci*.

The following Recit. (No. 43) contains an example
of Bach's literalness which the English Bible text
obscures. The word ' Pavement ' is translated in the
German version ' Hochpflaster ', High (upper) Pavement. With simple realism Bach approaches it by
leaping a sixth and descends from it by jumping a
fifth :

Ex. 25.

the High Pave - ment

Pilate's ' Behold your King ! ' is answered (No. 44)
in sharp, angry monosyllables, ' Hence, hence with
Him ! ', while in the first four bars the Continuo
sounds the subject which supported the cry, ' Jesus
of Nazareth ' in Nos. 3 and 5 :

Ex. 26.

With the word ' Crucify ', first heard in bar 4,

the rhythm of crucifixion (Ex. 21) enters and with increasing insistence dominates the movement (from this point a reconstruction of No. 36) to its close. The voices alternate their peremptory 'Hence, hence!' and the shout 'Crucify!' with its associated and sinister rhythm. For the last seven bars that cry alone is heard, while the Strings hammer out the fatal formula. The Flutes and Oboes are *con voci* and the second Oboe is *d'amore*.

No. 46, 'We have no King but Caesar', repeats Nos. 3, 5, and 29, and is accompanied by the same theme of malevolent pursuit (Ex. 6). The orchestra is normal, except that the second Oboe is *d'amore*.

Jesus passes to Calvary bearing His Cross. In the following Aria (No. 48) Zion (a Bass Voice) summons the faithful to follow Him thither. As usual, Bach indicates the act of hastening by a series of rapid passages in imitation. Handel, in his setting of Brockes's Passion, adopted the same device here:

Ex. 27.

At bars 82 and 85 of Bach's movement the word 'Flügel' (pinions) is accompanied by an upward rush of the Violins and Viola in unison, and on almost their every occurrence 'eilt' (haste) and 'flieht' (fly) are similarly illustrated.

The last Scene opens. The Crucifixion is accomplished, but Pilate's superscription excites the protest of the Jews (No. 50). The Chorus, 'Write thou not King of the Jews', is an adaptation of No. 34. Spitta criticizes Bach's repetition of its music to a text so

incongruous. In fact there is subtlety in the association of the Jews' protest with music which lately
had expressed their derisory homage to the ' King of
the Jews '. The orchestra is normal, but only the
Flutes and Oboes have independent parts.

Unlike the St. Matthew Passion, Bach interpolates
a Choral (No. 52) at this point. The words are the
third stanza of Valerius Herberger's funerary hymn,
' Valet will ich dir geben ' (1613), the melody by
Melchior Teschner (1613).

In No. 54 Bach pictures a nocturnal bivouac of
soldiers near the dying Saviour. They have robbed
Him of His vesture and in monotonous repetition,
which declares their insensitiveness, declaim an ani-
mated fugal theme :

Ex. 28.

Come now, let us not di - vide . . . . . . it.

The danger of too minute a glossing of Bach's text is
apparent when we find the semiquaver subject in the
Violoncelli :

Ex. 29.

interpreted by one writer as the rattling dice, and by
another as the Saviour's seamless robe ! The other
instruments are *con voci*. The orchestra is normal, but
the second Oboe is *d'amore*.

The Saviour's thought for His mother (No. 55) is
followed by a Choral (No. 56), which concludes the
Scene. The words are the twentieth stanza of Stockmann's hymn, to the melody already heard in No. 20.

VII. THE END

No. 57 (Recit.) :
St. John xix. 27–30 (' It is finished ').

No. 58 (Aria : Alto) (*Viola da Gamba, Cont., and Organ*) :

> 'Tis finished now !
> Sweet rest that comes to wearied mortals !
> This night of woe
> Doth draw my gaze beyond earth's portals,
> Where Judah's Hero bends His bow
> And Victor stands.   'Tis finished now !

No. 59 (Recit.) :
St. John xix. 30 (The death of Christ).

No. 60 (Aria (Bass) and Choral) (*Cont. and Organ*) :

> Thou dearest Saviour, answer give me,
> Since now the Cross no longer wounds Thee—
> Thyself hast said, ' 'Tis finished '.
> Am I from death deliverèd ?
> Shall I, through Thine own pain and merit,
> The joys of heaven inherit ?
> Shall all that lives redemption see ?
> Of speech Thy tortures have bereft Thee ;
> Yet dost incline Thy head,
> And say'st inclining, ' Yea '.

> *Jesu, Thou Who knewest death*
> *Livest now for ever.*
> *When I draw my latest breath*
> *Let nought from Thee sever.*
> *'Twas for me Thou suffered'st pain,*
> *Lord of Life and Glory ;*

What Thou willest is my gain,
More I do not ask Thee.

No. 61 (Recit.) :

St. Matthew xxvii. 51–2 (The Earthquake).

No. 62 (Arioso : Tenor) (*Strings, 2 Fl., 2 Ob. da caccia, Cont., and Organ*) :

> My heart, see how the world around
> Lord Jesu' suffering likewise shareth.
> The sun his beams in sorrow shroudeth.
> The Veil is riven, the rocks resound,
> The earth doth quake, the graves are opened,
> Their horror at His death betokened.
> And how, my heart, wilt show thy woe ?

No. 63 (Aria : Soprano) (*2 Fl., 2 Ob. da caccia, Cont., and Organ*) :

Dissolve now, my spirit, in torrents of weeping,
Thy Saviour lamenting.
To heaven and earth let thy sad message be said :
My Jesus is dead !

No. 64 (Recit.) :

St. John xix. 31–7 (They pierce His side).

No. 65 (Choral) (*as No. 7*) :

> *Grant us, Saviour, God's dear Son,*
> *By Thy bitter Passion,*
> *True to Thee our course to run,*
> *All our lives to fashion ;*
> *On Thy death and anguished woe*
> *Evermore reflecting,*

> And, though feeble is the flow,
> Thanks to Thee directing.

The Saviour's head sinks in death as He breathes the words (No. 57):

Ex. 30.

It is fin - ished.

An Alto voice takes up the phrase in the following Aria (No. 58), and the Viola da gamba obbligato heightens the atmosphere of grief that accompanies its repetition. With sudden contrast, at bar 20, the vision of Christ Triumphant effaces the Cross. The Strings, in soaring semiquavers, anticipate the Resurrection, though the rhythmic figure of the obbligato and Continuo holds Calvary still before us. The voice twice repeats the Saviour's dying words before the Evangelist (No. 59) announces the End.

The situation is treated less movingly than in the St. Matthew Passion, where the simple Choral (No. 72) that follows the Saviour's death is charged with deeper emotion. Here (No. 60) Bach is moved by Brockes's picture of the Daughter of Zion, prone before the dying Redeemer, begging an inclination of His sinking head to reassure her. He adds a stanza (the thirty-fourth) of Stockmann's hymn (cf. Nos. 20, 56), and sets Brockes's reconstructed text as a Fantasia upon it. Throughout the phrases of the Continuo, almost with exaggeration, end upon a sudden fall:

Ex. 31.

Spiccato.

Clearly the word ' neigest ' (literally, noddest) held
Bach's attention.   Although the movement is marked
Adagio, the almost cheerful tone of the Aria responds
to the Saviour's ' Yea '.

The description of the rending of the Temple Veil
(No. 61) is borrowed from St. Matthew's Gospel.
Bach's setting of the words in that Passion (No. 73)
is more elaborate.   But one observes how close in
curve the Evangelist's phrases are in both.

The Arioso (No. 62) and its following Aria (No. 63)
take up from the Recit. (No. 61) the demi-semiquaver
rhythm of trembling, while the Flutes and Oboes in
the Aria add an embroidery of expressive sighs :

Ex. 32.

The following Recit. (No. 64) contains a detail that
needs to be pointed out.   The Score adds a *piano* at
bar 4 over the words in parenthesis (' for the Sabbath
day was of all a high day ') and a *forte* over the words
that follow.   It was Bach's habit to mark *Adagio*
Recit. passages which he desired to distinguish in
the ordinary Bible narrative (e. g. No. 18, bar 11 ;
No. 49, bar 8), or quotations from the Old Testament
(e. g. No. 55, bar 3 ; No. 64, bars 26 and 28).   But
the passage under examination belongs to neither of
these categories.   It is matched by another in No. 66,
bar 3, where again the text marked *piano* is a
parenthesis ('but secretly for fear of the Jews').   They
indicate Bach's metriculous attention to his text.

The concluding Choral (No. 65) is the eighth stanza
of Michael Weisse's ' Christus, der uns selig macht '
(cf. No. 21).

VIII. THE BURIAL

No. 66 (Recit.) :

St. John xix. 38–end (The burial of Christ).

No. 67 (Chorus) (*Strings, 2 Fl., 2 Ob., Cont., and Organ*) :

Now rest Thy members worn and holy ;
No longer henceforth I'll bemoan Thee.
So, sleep and bring me soon to rest !
The grave that doth my Lord enclose
Nor grief nor sorrow's mourning knows ;
To heaven above it leads, and hell is dispossessed.

No. 68 (Choral) (*as No. 7*) :

Lord, let Thy blessed angels come
At my last end, when life is done,
To bear my soul to heaven.
Asleep within the quiet tomb
I'll calm await Thy day of doom,
All fear and pain far driven.
One day from death awaken me,
To let my soul Thy beauty see
In all Thy glory, God's dear Son,
Who hath for me salvation won.
Lord Jesus Christ,
O hear Thou me, receive my prayer,
Who evermore Thy praise declare !

Over the Saviour now at rest Zion and the faithful sing a last farewell. Though actually He was not interred in ordinary burial, here (No. 68), as in the St. Matthew Passion (No. 78), Bach depicts the

I   D

mourners lowering the Saviour's body into the grave
by descending phrases :

Ex. 33.

The movement is a prolonged lament and leave-taking.
' Flowing passages in quavers on the strings ', Spitta
comments,[1] ' sink softly down to the lowest depths,
mingling with the tearful tenderness of the vocal
parts like the dull, slow fall of clods on the coffin.'

It is a curious fact, not observed by other writers,
that here, as in the corresponding movement in the
St. Matthew Passion, Bach found his theme among
the instrumental compositions of his Cöthen period.
There is a clear reminiscence of the Rondeau of the
Overture in B minor for Flute and Strings [2] in the
opening theme of the Chorus (No. 67) :

Ex. 34.   (No. 67.)

RONDEAU.

---

[1] *Op. cit.* ii. 534.   [2] *B. G.* xxxi (1), p. 32.

Between the Choruses of farewell in the two Passions there are other resemblances. They are alike in tonality and measure, and between their middle sections there is a remarkable likeness :

Ex. 35.

The St. John Chorus is upon a smaller plan than its counterpart, but it is charged with more intimate emotion. For that reason, perhaps, Bach preferred to conclude with a congregational hymn. The words of No. 68 are the third stanza of Martin Schalling's ' Herzlich lieb hab' ich dich, O Herr ' (1571). The anonymous melody was first published in 1577.

II. *Picander's Passion*

(1725)

PICANDER's printed works [1] include a Passion libretto
entitled *Erbauliche Gedancken auf den Grünen Donners-
tag und Charfreytag über den Leidenden Jesum. In
einem Oratorio entworffen,* 1725. It contains about
250 rhymed lines arranged in 32 movements—9 Arias,
5 Soliloquies (a term borrowed from Hunold-Menan-
tes), 1 Arioso, 2 Chorals, 12 Recits. for the Evangelist,
and 3 Choruses. The text is modelled upon that of
Brockes, published thirteen years before, but is shorter
than and inferior to its model. Besides the Evangelist,
the characters are Zion (whose voice utters the opening Choruses of Parts I and II), Peter (3 Arias), John
(1 Aria), the Soul (3 Soliloquies and 3 Arias), Mary the
Mother of Christ (1 Soliloquy), and the Faithful
(Chor der gläubigen Seelen) (1 Chorus). The Saviour
speaks only twice, once in each Part,[2] in two Arias.
The Passion story is outlined in the barest detail.
Following Zion's opening summons to the faithful
(getreue Seelen) to embrace the Saviour before His
Passion (vor seinem Ende), the Evangelist briefly
records the Institution of the Holy Supper. John
then apostrophizes (Aria) the gift of heavenly food.
A short Recit. transfers the Scene to the Mount of

---

[1] Printed in Spitta (German edition), ii. 873 f.
[2] The libretto actually is not divided.

Olives, where the Soul soliloquizes on the Saviour's Agony :

> Ja ! sieh, mein Hertz,
> Wie ihm der Schweiss herunterwerts
> Durch seine Schläfe dringt
> Und blutend auf die Erde fällt.

(Yea, my heart, see how the sweat drops from His temples and, mingled with blood, falls to earth.)

Judas accomplishes his treachery, and is hotly rated by Peter :

> Verdammter Verräther, wo hast du dein Hertze ?

(Accursed betrayer, hast thou a heart ?)

In ten words the Scene passes abruptly to the palace of Caiaphas, where the Soul soliloquizes on the Saviour's desertion by His disciples :

> Die Nacht verklagt den Sonnenschein,
> Und niemand ist der ihn vertritt.
> Die Jünger sind von dir geflogen,
> Der eine hier,
> Der andre dort.

(Night accuses the sun. No one stands by Him. His disciples have fled, some here, some there.)

As later in the St. Matthew Passion (No. 23), the sixth stanza of Paul Gerhardt's ' O Haupt voll Blut und Wunden ' is inserted at this point.

To Peter's denial of Christ, which follows, Picander gives the same disproportionate prominence as Brockes: two Recits. and two *da capo* Arias are devoted to it. The Evangelist next narrates the incident of the false witnesses, and then, for the first time, Jesus speaks, in an Aria :

> Aus Liebe will ich alles dulden,
> Aus Liebe sterb' ich vor die Welt.

(For love I endure all things. For the world lovingly I give my life.)

Six lines narrate the Scourging, and are followed
by a Chorus in which Zion summons her daughters
(' Kommt, ihr Töchter ', as in the St. Matthew
Passion, No. 1) to witness the Saviour's martyrdom.
A Soliloquy and Arioso follow, after which the
Evangelist describes the procession to Calvary in
words characteristic of Picander's indelicacy :

> Die Weiber folgten nach,
> Wiewohl sie in den Thränen-Güssen
> Nicht gehen, sondern schwimmen müssen.

(The women follow Him, not on foot, but swimming in the
torrent of their tears.)

Jesus (Aria) addresses the weeping women—His
second and final utterance—and Mary replies in a
piteous Soliloquy. A Choral follows, after which the
Evangelist briefly describes the Crucifixion. In an
Aria the Soul adjures the Saviour not to drink the
proffered vinegar :

> Nimm es nicht, mein ander Leben.
> Was sie dir zu trincken geben
> Ist ein saurer bittrer Wein.

(Touch not what is offered Thee ; it is sour and bitter wine.)

Curtly, in four lines, the Evangelist narrates the
End :

> Und um die neundte Stunde
> Rief unser Heyl mit lautem Munde
> Es ist vollbracht !
> Da gab der Geist dem Leibe gute Nacht.

(At the ninth hour the Saviour called with a loud voice, It is
finished, and gave up the ghost.)

As in Brockes and the St. John Passion, the Saviour's
' It is finished ' furnishes the text for a reflective
interlude. Picander here inserts a Soliloquy and Aria
for the Soul, after which the Evangelist narrates the

intervention of Joseph of Arimathaea. The libretto
ends, like the St. Matthew Passion, with a ' Chorus of
the Faithful ', whose lines Picander adapted in 1728
for that work. The emendations of the later text are
shown in italic : lines omitted from it are within
square brackets :

Wir setzen uns $\left\{\begin{array}{l}\textit{mit Thränen}\\ \text{bey deinem Grabe}\end{array}\right\}$ nieder,

Und ruffen dir im $\left\{\begin{array}{l}\textit{Grabe}\\ \text{Tode}\end{array}\right\}$ zu:

Ruhe sanffte, sanffte ruh !

$\left\{\begin{array}{l}\textit{Ruht, ihr}\\ \text{Erquicket euch, ihr}\end{array}\right\}$ ausgesognen Glieder,

[Verschlafet die erlittne Wuth] ;

Ruhet sanffte, sanffte ruht !

[Unsre Thränen
Werden sich stets nach dir sehnen ;]

$\left\{\begin{array}{l}\textit{Euer Grab und}\\ \text{Endlich soll dein}\end{array}\right\}$ Leichen-Stein

Soll dem ängstlichen Gewissen

Ein bequemes Ruhe-Kissen

$\left\{\begin{array}{l}\textit{Und der Seelen Ruhstatt}\\ \text{Unser weiches Bette}\end{array}\right\}$ sein,

$\left\{\begin{array}{l}\textit{Höchst}\\ \text{Recht}\end{array}\right\}$ vergnügt schlummern $\left\{\begin{array}{l}\textit{da die Augen}\\ \text{wir auf solchem}\end{array}\right\}$ ein.

Did Bach set Picander's text to music ? It cannot
have satisfied him, though its constructive superiority
to his St. John libretto is admitted. The Passion
story is told in meagrest outline ; its incidents are
presented without devotional emphasis ; and Chorals
are almost entirely excluded. The abandonment of
the Bible text might also be remarked as a blemish
in Bach's eyes were it not that in 1731 he accepted
a libretto similarly distinguished. Spitta [1] finds an
argument for his association with Picander's text in
the exclusion of 'O Mensch, bewein'' from the St. John

[1] *Op. cit.* ii. 507.

Passion upon its second performance in 1727. Since
the St. Matthew Passion, into which that movement
was finally incorporated, was not yet written, there
must have been some other reason for Bach's omission
of it in 1727. That he had used it already in 1725
might account for its absence in 1727. On the other
hand, other reasons may be supposed for its exclusion.
It is certainly not improbable that at the outset of his
Leipzig career Bach may have been willing to please
his constituents by collaborating with Picander in the
production of a Passion of the popular Brockes type.
His association with him in 1728 and again in 1731
in works of similar character supports the supposition
that the text of 1725 was also written for Bach's use.

'THE MUSICAL PILGRIM'

General Editor   Dr. Arthur Somervell

BACH

The Passions

BOOK II : 1729–31

BY

CHARLES SANFORD TERRY

Litt.D. (Cantab.), Hon. Mus.D. (Edin.)
Hon. D.Litt. (Dunelm.), Hon. LL.D. (Glasg.)

GREENWOOD PRESS, PUBLISHERS
WESTPORT, CONNECTICUT

Prefatory Note

THIS volume and its predecessor exceed the require-
ments of those whose interest in Bach's Passions is
confined to the two that survive. I preferred to treat
the subject exhaustively, because there is no other
book on the subject, in English or foreign literature,
accessible to the student, whose needs this Series
serves. Lack of space prevents me from tracing the
development of Passion music to Bach's epoch. For
that preliminary chapter I refer the reader to my
article in the new (3rd) edition of Grove.

The analyses of the St. John and St. Matthew
Passions intentionally are non-technical. Their principal aim is to stimulate the listener's interest by
revealing the intimate relationship between Bach's
music and his libretti. The *Leitmotif* was as much
his characteristic as it was Wagner's a century later.

New translations of the texts of the St. John and
St. Matthew Passions are provided ; those in English
use being unreliable and misleading. These are
metrically true to the originals and do not violate
Bach's declamation. In the Recitatives especially, but
not exclusively, English editors have taken liberties
with Bach's text which are the less excusable because
they are gratuitous.

Book I, in addition to an Introduction outlining

4 *Prefatory Note*

the conditions under which Bach produced his Passions at Leipzig, deals with the St. John Passion and Picander's text written in 1725. Book II, besides a short Conclusion, treats the St. Matthew and St. Mark Passions and discusses the St. Luke Passion in relation to Bach's asserted authorship.

Many will welcome the information that Miniature Scores of the St. Matthew and St. John Passions are published respectively by Eulenburg and the Vienna Philharmonischer Verlag.

C. S. T.

King's College,
Old Aberdeen, *September* 1925.

CONTENTS

BOOK II

III. *The St. Matthew Passion*

(1729)

BACH produced the St. Matthew Passion in St. Thomas's on Good Friday (15 April) 1729, a sacred work to which only the Mass in B minor is comparable, the deepest expression of devotional feeling that the art of music affords, so intimately felt, unfolded with such sensitive emphasis and dramatic feeling, that, as Pirro [1] remarks, the music seems embroidered with tears and coloured with flames and blood.

Picander wrote the libretto in 1728 and published it at Easter, 1729. Bach certainly was at work upon it in the autumn of 1728 and had finished some movements before 19 November, when his patron, Leopold of Anhalt-Cöthen, died. In his memory Bach forthwith was commissioned to compose *Trauer-musik*, which was performed at Cöthen probably early in January 1729. Engaged at the moment on the composition of the Passion, Bach was not at leisure to produce an original work. He therefore invited Picander to fit new words to such of the Passion movements already completed as it was convenient to employ. Picander produced the following libretto :

[1] *Op. cit.*, p. 183.

Trauermusik

1. Arie (Tutti) :

Klagt, Kinder, klagt es aller Welt,
Lasst es den fernen Gränzen wissen,
Wie euer Schatten eingerissen,
Wie euer Landesvater fällt.

2. Arie (No. 10) :

Weh und Ach
Kränkt die Seelen tausendfach,
Und die Augen treuer Liebe
Werden wie ein heller Bach
Bei entstandnem Wetter trübe.

3. 'Wir haben einen Gott, der da hilft, und einen Herrn Herrn,
der vom Tode errettet' (Ps. lxviii. 20).

4. Arie (No. 48) :

Erhalte mich,
Gott, in der Hälfte meiner Tage,
Schone doch,
Meiner Seele fällt das Joch
Jämmerlich.

5. Arie (No. 58) :

Mit Freuden,
Mit Freuden sei die Welt verlassen,
Der Tod kommt mir recht tröstlich für ;
Ich will meinen Gott umfassen,
Dieser hilft und bleibt bei mir,
Wenn sich Geist und Glieder scheiden.

6. Arie (No. 66) :

Lass, Leopold, dich nicht begraben.
Es ist dein Land, das nach dir ruft ;
Du sollst ein' ewig sanfte Gruft
In unser aller Herzen haben.

7. Arie (No. 29) :

Wird auch gleich nach tausend Zähren
Sich das Auge wieder klären,
Denkt doch unser Herz an dich ;
Deine Huld,

Die wir nicht zu preisen wissen,
Und Geduld
Blieb uns gleichfalls ewiglich,
Wenn du nur nicht sterben müssen.

8. Arie (No. 26) : à 2 Chören : 1. Die Sterblichen.
    2. Die Auserwählten.

1. Geh, Leopold, zu deiner Ruhe

2. Und schlummre nur ein wenig ein.

1. Unsre Ruh,
    So sonst Niemand, ausser du,
    Wird nun zugleich mit dir begraben.

2. Der Geist soll sich im Himmel laben
    Und königlich am Glanze sein.

9. Arie (No. 75) :

Bleibet nur in eurer Ruh,
Ihr erblassten Fürstenglieder ;
Doch verwandelt nach der Zeit
Unser Leid
In vergnügte Freude wieder,
Schliesst uns auch die Thränen zu.

10. Arie (No. 19) :

Hemme dein gequältes Kränken,
Spare dich der guten Zeit,
Die den Kummer wird versenken
Und der Lust die Hände beut ;
Schmerzen, die am grössten sein,
Halten desto eher ein.

11. Arie (Tutti) (No. 78) :

Die Augen sehn nach deiner Leiche,
Der Mund ruft in die Gruft hinein :
Schlafe süsse, ruhe fein,
Labe dich im Himmelreich !
Nimm die letzte Gute Nacht
Von den Deinen, die dich lieben,
Die sich über dich betrüben,
Die dein Herze werth geacht,
Wo dein Ruhm sich unsterblich hat gemacht.

Bach, no doubt, composed original music for No. 3. But for the remaining movements he used old material. The opening Chorus of the *Trauer-Ode* of 1727 (which he inserted later into the St. Mark Passion) was fitted to No. 1. For all the rest he utilized adapted movements of the as yet unfinished St. Matthew Passion, their numbers being shown above in brackets. Bach's insensibility in adapting his music to incongruous texts is one of the puzzles of his character. On the other hand, it must be remembered that his duty as Cantor was to compose music and not merely to select it, a burden of responsibility which explains, and perhaps condones, his indifference. The Score of the *Trauermusik* was known to J. N. Forkel in 1802.[1] It has long since disappeared.

The libretto of the St. Matthew Passion, like that of the *Trauermusik*, appears to have been written under Bach's direction. Picander's facile but insincere pen was available to supply his technical literary deficiencies. But the general treatment of the text was his own, and the choice and distribution of the Chorals, so admirably selected and placed, must also be attributed to him. Picander took so little responsibility for them that, whereas he published his 1725 and 1731 Passion texts in full, his St. Matthew omits everything except the lyrics that came from his pen.[2]

Picander's *Texte zur Passions-Music, nach dem Evangelisten Matthäo, am Char-Freytage bey der Vesper in der Kirche zu St. Thomä* is in two Parts, headed respectively, like the St. Mark Passion, 'Vor der Predigt' and 'Nach der Predigt'.[3] As in Picander's 1725 text, it introduces the conventional Daughter of

[1] *J. S. Bach* (trans. Terry), p. 90.
[2] Printed in *B.G.* iv, p. xxxii.
[3] ' Before the Sermon ' ; ' After the Sermon '.

Zion and Chorus of the Faithful, who appear in seven
movements—Nos. 1, 25, 26, 33, 36, 70, and 77.
Picander seems to have borrowed ideas from other
sources. In No. 9 of the St. Matthew Passion the
voice sings :

> Yet still to me the favour deign,
> That tears now from my eyes swift flowing
> Sweet unction on Thee may be pouring.

The thought seems to have been suggested by Salomo
Franck's *Madrigalische Seelen-Lust* (Arnstadt, 1697) :

> Hab' ich nicht Narden-Fluth,
> So netz' ich dich mit meinen Thränen-Bächen.[1]

A stronger suggestion of extraneous influence is dis-
covered in No. 74, whose text appears to have been
inspired by the same author's ' Auf Christi Begräbniss
gegen Abend '.[2]

Bach's literary collaboration with Picander produced a libretto of exceptional length and dramatic
force. Its foundation—chapters xxvi and xxvii of
St. Matthew's Gospel—consists of 141 as against 82
Bible verses in St. John's. It contains 27 lyrical
numbers as against 12 in the earlier Passion, 12 independent Choral movements as against 11. The Score
is laid out upon a scale the more remarkable in view
of Bach's contemporary complaint regarding the
inadequate vocal and orchestral materials at his dis-
posal, which is dated 23 August 1730. The work
requires two separate Choirs, each supported by its
own Orchestra of Strings, Flutes, Oboes, Cont.,
Organ. According to Bach's statement, each vocal
part required at least one *concertist* (a person capable

---

[1] Quoted in Spitta (German edition), ii. 368.
[2] It is too long to quote. Spitta prints it *op. cit.*, p. 175.

of singing solos) and two *ripienists*, three voices in all.
Excepting one short passage (No. 39), the whole of
the Bible Recitatives are allotted to Choir I, whose
members therefore sang the music of Jesus (Bass), the
Evangelist (Tenor), Peter (Bass), Judas (Bass), Pilate
(Bass), two Priests (Basses), Pilate's wife (Soprano),
and two Maids (Soprani). In Choir II the only
Biblical characters are the two False Witnesses (Alto,
Tenor). Arias or Ariosos are sung by each of the
voices in both Choirs. Their composition, therefore,
may have been as follows : [1]

Choir I		Choir II
Soprano C C R R	⎫	C R R R ⎫
Alto C R R R	⎬ = 18	C R R R ⎬ = 16
Tenor C (Evang.) C R R R	⎪	C R R R ⎪
Bass C (Jesus) C C (or R) R R	⎭	C R R R ⎭

Regarding the Orchestra, Bach states his require-
ments as '2 or even 3' first and second Violins,
4 Violas, 2 Violoncelli, 1 Violone. To these must be
added 2 Flutes and 2 Oboes, a minimum of fifteen
players in each body. Probably the occasional instruments used in Choir I—Viola da gamba, 2 Oboe d'amore,
2 Oboe da caccia—were played by the other instrumentalists : only the Oboe d'amore are also needed in Choir II
(No. 35). The two Orchestras were composed,
partly of professional players maintained by the
municipality, partly of scholars of the Thomasschule,
partly of Bach's Collegium Musicum (Musical Society),
which was in close touch with the University.

[1] These conjectural lists tally with a 'Chorordnung' for 1744–5
which shows that the two principal choirs on which Bach relied
for performances of concerted music numbered 34 in all : *Sop.* 9 ;
Alto 6 ; *Tenor* 8 ; *Bass* 11. The disproportionate strength of
the Tenors and Basses is explained by the fact that Bach's singers
were young.

In the employment of these complementary forces, Bach worked upon a considered plan. The two Choirs lose their separate identity and speak in common utterance very rarely and with specific intention. Excluding the Chorals, in which the two bodies of singers and instrumentalists invariably combine, there are only seven movements in which the two become one. The first, No. 35, concludes Part I, and needs no comment. The remaining six are in Part II. In Nos. 54 and 59 (two) the two Choirs jointly voice the vindictive enmity that assailed the Saviour. In No. 73 they unite to express the awe that drew from His persecutors the admission, 'Truly this was the Son of God.' In No. 67 a tumultuous mob round the Cross becomes united as it flings the taunt, 'If He be King of Israel, let Him come down!' In No. 76 the two bodies unite in outraged recollection of the Saviour's 'blasphemy'.

Outside these examples, Bach invests each Choir with a separate individuality. The Disciples, the inmost circle of the Christian community, are invariably represented by Choir I (Nos. 7, 14, 15); the larger congregation, styled by Picander 'Die Gläubigen' (the Faithful), by Choir II. Whenever Choir II in that character is associated with Choir I as a separate body, the latter invariably is the voice of the Daughter of Zion, whether a Solo voice or a Chorus (Nos. 1, 25, 26, 33, 36, 70, 77).[1] While Bach allows the priests, scribes, and populace to speak with the full strength of his resources (Nos. 5, 43, 45, 50, 54, 62, 67), he never associates the two Christian bodies in a Chorus except in four movements which

---

[1] In Nos. 47 and 71 the two Choirs represent small groups of Jews.

voice a wider emotion (Nos. 1, 33, 35, 78). By this
device Bach expresses the numerical minority of the
Christian community.

The Original Score of the St. Matthew Passion is
in the Preuss. Staatsbibliothek (P. 25), where also are
the original Parts (St. 110) which formerly belonged
to the Berlin Sing-Akademie. The Score, a facsimile
of which was published by the Insel-Verlag, Leipzig,
in 1922, is in Bach's autograph throughout. The
title-page is inscribed *Passio Domini nostri J. C.
secundum Evangelistam Matthaeum. Poesìa per Dominum Henrici alias Picander dictus. Musica di G. S.
Bach. Prima Parte.* The first Chorus is headed
' J[esu] J[uva]. Passio D. N. J. C. secundū Matthaeum '
and below No. 35 is inscribed ' Fine della Pma
Parte '. The second Part has a separate title-page,
inscribed *Passionis D. N. J. C. secundum Matthaeum a due Cori. Parte Seconda.* Its first Chorus
(No. 36) is headed ' J. J. Pars 2da Passionis Xti
secundū Matthaeum a due Chori per G. S. Bach '.
The foot of the final page bears Bach's usual dedication, ' SDGl ' (To God alone be the praise). The
Autograph contains 166 folio pages, of which the last
of Parts I and II are blank. The writing is exceed-
ingly clear and the manuscript is evidently a fair
copy ; there is hardly a correction in the whole of it.
The Choral melody of No. 1 and the Bible text
throughout are inserted in red ink. The Continuo
is unfigured, an omission supplied by the Parts. The
Strings' accompaniment to the Saviour's words is
written out in full Score. Only the voice parts of the
Chorals are given. No. 46 is headed ' Stromenti
concordant ' ; otherwise the Score affords no indication of their instrumentation. The Parts supply the
omission.

The general appearance of the Autograph supports
the conclusion that it was written towards the end of
Bach's life, probably *circa* 1747–8. The first state of
the Score exists in a copy once owned by Bach's
pupil, Joh. Philipp Kirnberger (1721–83), now in the
Preuss. Staatsbibliothek (Amalien. 6 and 7), which can
be dated *c.* 1741. Its value is in its testimony to a fact
hitherto not observed : Part I ends with the simple
four-part Choral, ' Jesum lass ich nicht von mir ',
printed in *B. G.* xli. 201.[1] Hence, we can conclude
positively that Bach put ' O Mensch, bewein' dein'
Sünde gross ' into its present position quite at the
end of his life.

In his Preface to the Bachgesellschaft edition of the
St. Matthew Passion, Julius Rietz (1812–77) supposes
that, in writing distinct Organ parts for the two
Choirs, Bach prescribed an ideal which St. Thomas's
resources could not realize. In fact, as has been
shown, two Organs stood in the church until 1740,
when the smaller was removed in a useless condition.
Custos Rost expressly records the performance of the
Passion music in 1736 ' mit beÿde Orgeln ', a circumstance that points to the St. Matthew Passion having
been repeated that year. Six years earlier (1730) the
Rückpositiv of the larger Organ had received a key-
board of its own. Therefore in 1729, when the
St. Matthew Passion was first performed, one Organ
did duty for both Choirs. It may be concluded that
the St. Matthew Passion was sung for the first time
in 1736 with the full orchestral resources Bach
demanded.

Rietz is inaccurate also in his conclusion that the
Bible Recitatives were accompanied on the Cembalo

---

[1] No. 255 of 'Bach's Four-part Chorals: Complete and
Critical Edition ' (Ed. Terry : O.U.P.).

or Clavier. It is true that the **B. G.** Score specifies
their accompaniments throughout for the ' Continuo '
and all the other movements for ' Organ and Continuo '.   But they are found in the ' Continuo pro
Organo ' part, and must have been played on that
instrument. No ' Continuo pro Cembalo ' part for
Choir I is extant, a fact which does not establish its
non-existence in Bach's time.

PART I

I. PROLOGUE[1]

No. 1 (Chorus) (*Strings, 2 Fl., 2 Ob., Cont., and
Organ in each Choir*) :
   Choir I.   Come, O daughters, swell my mourning.
               See Him !
   Choir II. Whom ?
   Choir I.   Your Lord and King. See Him !
   Choir II. How ?
   Choir I.   E'en as a Lamb. Mark it !
   Choir II. What ?
   Choir I.   His patience rare. Look !
   Choir II. Whereon ?

[1] The sectional headings adopted here are not in the original
text.

Choir I. Our sinning sore.
                 Look on Him ! For love of us
                 He His Cross to Calvary's bearing.

Choral. *O Lamb of God, pure, spotless,*
           Who on the Cross once did'st languish,
           Who suffered man's unkindness
           And knew the bitterest anguish ;
           Our sin Thou bearest for us,
           Else hell had triumphed o'er us ;
           Have mercy on us, O Jesu.

No. 2 (Recit.) :
St. Matthew xxvi. 1–2 (Christ foretells His Crucifixion).

No. 3 (Choral) (*Strings, 2 Fl., 2 Ob., Cont., and Organ*) :
Beloved Jesu, how hast Thou defaulted ?
For what offence has judgement harsh been uttered ?
What deed hast done ? of what hast made confession,
Or owned transgression ?

In conception and composition the movement is one of the largest and most impressive pictures in Bach's gallery. In the foreground a band of Roman soldiers ; in their midst the Man of Sorrows staggering under the Cross's burden : a sad procession moving forward slowly : Zion and her daughters in the distance awaiting it expectant. For the first seventeen bars the two Orchestras (in unison until bar 14) unite in a march-like rhythm heard above a throbbing pedal point which typifies the weary Saviour :

Ex. 36.

At bar **17** Zion adds her voice on a theme whose opening wail rises a full octave, in counterpoint with the march-like theme of approach, a subject whose chromatic structure bespeaks the bitterest woe:

Ex. 37.

The procession sweeps on, a swelling concourse, amid increasing lamentation as Zion sees before her the Cross and its Bearer, the Lamb led to the sacrificial altar. At the word, a celestial Choir adores the Lamb of God in Nikolaus Decius's version of the 'Agnus Dei' (1531). In the Autograph its melody (1542) is inserted below the voices in each Choir, without words, and on a separate stave braced to the Continuo. It is, however, unquestionable that Bach intended it to be sung; the words of the Choral are printed in Picander's text, and a separate part for the singers (which also includes the melody of No. 35) exists in Bach's own hand. The recent suggestion of

Wilhelm Werker [1] that the melody was rendered by a few choir-boys in the Chancel is quite unwarranted.

At bar 57, above the Organ's persisting rhythm, both Orchestras, with Choir II, develop a new, alert subject :

Ex. 38.

The inquisitive phrase, inspired by the word ' Wohin ' (Whereon) is thrown from one Orchestra to the other, leaping upward with the urgency of a question, ' Is it I ', as Zion bids her hearers find within themselves the cause of the Saviour's doom.   Inverted :

Ex. 39.

the phrase expresses the quintessence of remorse as,
in the final bars, both Choirs acclaim the Lamb of
God.

It is a merit in St. Matthew's text, absent in
St. John's, that the voice of the Saviour is heard at
once announcing the impending tragedy.   Accompanied by the instrumental nimbus that illuminates
His every utterance save one, Jesus (No. 2) foretells His
Crucifixion on a phrase whose structure anticipates
the cry of His enemies in No. 54 :

Ex. 40.

Spitta,[1] who was little inclined to exaggerate the
pictorial significance of Bach's musical themes, finds
in this one the figure of a Cross whose horizontal
arms are spanned by the outmost notes of the second
(No. 54) illustration above.   Clearly the notes B D A
form an angle of acute poignancy and express the
agony of the Cross's victim.   In the St. John Passion
(No. 1) the thought of the Crucifixion summons a
similarly curved phrase to Bach's mind :

Ex. 41.
Bar 58.

As in the St. John Passion, Bach employs Johann
Heermann's ' Herzliebster Jesu, was hast du ver-

[1] *Op. cit.* ii. 549.

brochen' (stanza i) as the first Choral. It is set to
Johann Crüger's melody (1640), and occurs again twice
(Nos. 25, 55).

II. THE CONSPIRACY

Nos. 4–5 (Recit. and Chorus) :

St. Matthew xxvi. 3–5 (The rulers conspire against
Christ).

The Prologue is ended ; the Saviour has announced
the approaching tragedy ; the Church has uttered
her subdued commentary. In the palace of Caiaphas
the Saviour's capture is planned. No. 5, the first of
the incisive choruses which distinguish the St. Matthew
Passion from the St. John, puts an indignant emphasis
on the words which they hardly bear. St. Mark
(xiv. 2) confirms St. Matthew's text. St. John is
silent. But St. Luke (xxii. 2), instead of ' lest there be
an uproar ', writes ' for they feared the people '.
A close student of the Bible, Bach expresses the anxiety
and fear St. Luke's text declares. Over an agitated
theme in the Continuo, now rising, now falling, as
the outcry waxes and wanes :

Ex. 42.

the assemblage, divided and distracted, reveals its
fear of the populace, combining at the fifth bar in
a realistic figure on the word ' uproar '. The
Orchestra is as in No. 1.

III. BETHANY

Nos. 6–8 (Recits. and Chorus) :
St. Matthew xxvi. 6–13 (The anointing of Christ).

No. 9 (Recit. : Alto) (2 *Fl., Cont., and Organ*) :
    O dearest Saviour mine,
    See ! Thy disciples foolish chide Thee
    Because this woman's love
    With unguents for the grave
    Thy body maketh ready.
    Yet, still to me the favour deign,
    The tears now from my eyes swift flowing
    Sweet unction on Thy head be pouring.

No. 10 (Aria : Alto) (*as No.* 9) :
    Sin's dull grief
    Bids my erring heart to break.
    See, my tear-drops, hotly falling,
    Sweetest, soothing spices make,
    Dearest Jesu, for Thy suffering !

The Twelve are assembled at Bethany. Bach gives
sublime tenderness to the Saviour's commendation of
Mary Magdalene (No. 8). By contrast there is acerbity
in the disciples' remonstrance (No. 7) :

Ex. 43.

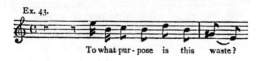

and indignation in their fugal :

Ex. 44.

For this oint-ment, for this oint-ment might have been sold

The Flutes (the Orchestra is normal) add a carping note :

Ex. 45.

The following Recit. (No. 8) is of great significance. At bar 12 the Saviour foretells the new Gospel's victory as a world religion. The Violins, having subsided into the grave at Christ's reference to His burial, soar upwards on a chord of D minor :

Ex. 46.
Vn. i.

rising whose significance is shown in No. 17, where a similar theme is associated with the promise of the New Testament :

Ex. 47.

This   is   my   blood   of the new Tes - ta - ment

Two reflective movements close the scene. No. 9,

characteristic of the St. Matthew Passion, is outside
the category of formal Recitative, its essentials being
a free, declamatory voice part with instrumental
accompaniment, well suited to Picander's rhymed
prose. Of this type, too, are Nos. 18, 25, 28, 40, 57,
61, 65, 69, 74. Both Recit. and Aria (Nos. 9, 10) are
dominated by the *motif* of tears and grief of which
their texts speak :

Ex. 48.

The phrasing is Bach's, forming a succession of
emotional periods, each punctuated by a tear-drop.
The pictorial device is particularly graphic in the
second part of the Aria :

Ex. 49.

Bach recalled the opening of No. 10 when he wrote the *Kyrie* of the Mass in B minor a few years later. In both he sees the penitent oppressed by the load of sin :

Ex. 50.   No. 10.

Sin's   dull grief,   sin's   dull   grief

Ky · ri - e

IV. JUDAS

No. 11 (Recit.) :

St. Matthew xxvi. 14–16 (Judas's treachery).

No. 12 (Aria : Soprano) (*Strings, 2 Fl., Cont., and Organ*) :

> Break in woe, O loving heart !
> For, a son whom Thou didst nourish,
> One, a friend whom Thou didst cherish,
> Seeks his Master to entangle,
> Yea would like a serpent strangle.

On a phrase harsh and strident (No. 11) Judas sells his soul. The following Aria (No. 12) is one of only three in the work not preceded by a Recitative of the kind considered above under No. 9. The others are Nos. 48 and 51. It may be merely a coincidence that all three comment on acts of betrayal. The Aria pulses

with sorrow in the idiom of Ex. 48. Spitta [1] finds
confusion of thought in the stanza. But Picander's
intention is not doubtful.

V. THE INSTITUTION OF THE HOLY SUPPER

Nos. 13–15 (Recits. and Choruses) :
St. Matthew xxvi. 17–22 (Christ foretells His
betrayal).

No. 16 (Choral) (*Strings, 2 Ob., Cont., and Organ*) :
>*'Tis I should show contrition,*
>*Deserving of perdition,*
>*And worthy deepest hell !*
>*The tortures that await Thee,*
>*The thongs that soon shall pain Thee,*
>*Myself should bear, I know full well.*

No. 17 (Recit.) :
St. Matthew xxvi. 23–9 (The Institution).

No. 18 (Recit. : Soprano) (2 *Ob. d'amore, Cont., and
Organ*) :
>Although in tears dissolves my heart,
>Since Jesus from me must depart,
>Yet still His bounty doth my soul uplift ;
>His Flesh and Blood, a costly gift,
>Bequeatheth He to mine own keeping.

---

[1] *Op. cit.* ii. 565.

As He while here on earth did guard His children,
Nor evil let approach them,
His love e'en now is never sleeping.

No. 19 (Aria : Soprano) (*as No.* 18) :

To Thee all my heart is given ;
Enter in, dear Lord, and dwell.
In Thy ways alone I've striven,
On earth nought I love so well.
Dearer too than heaven beside
Is my Lord Who loved and died.

With an abrupt change of tonality to G major from
the B minor of No. 12, Bach passes to the Upper
Chamber, creating an atmosphere of serenity and
expectant joy, of which the characteristic rhythm
(No. 13)  is
a factor. The short Chorus (No. 14), so different in
mood from No. 7, opens with a reiterated 'where ?'
Rising from the mediant to the dominant and thence
to the upper tonic, it reveals urgent expectancy :

Ex. 51.

Answered by a similarly questioning theme in the
Continuo :

Ex. 52.

it has an obvious relation to Exs. 46 and 47, and
connects the disciples' eagerness with the approaching
inauguration. The Chorus is bright and expectant,
a mood continued in the following Recit. (No. 15),
where the same tonality is maintained until the
Saviour's reference to the traitor Judas summons an
abrupt chord of B flat minor (bar 16).

The short Chorus (No. 15), marked by Bach *Allegro*,
is tinged with sad and eager anxiety. The short
phrase :

Ex. 53.

Lord,   is 't I?

is stated eleven times—thrice in each of the three
upper voices, twice in the Bass. Though Bach's
realism is more thorough—Judas's question is put
in No. 17—his treatment of the text is conventional.
Schütz (St. Matthew Passion) set it thus :

Ex. 54.

Another significant change of key brings us to the
Choral (No. 16), stanza v of Paul Gerhardt's ' O Welt,
ieh' hier dein Leben ' (1647), set to an originally

secular tune improbably attributed to Heinrich Isaak
(1539), heard again in No. 46.

Schweitzer [1] very truly observes, that if we have
once absorbed a Bible text in Bach's rhythm the
association is ineffaceable. The reflection is especially
true of St. Matthew's narrative of the Institution of
the Holy Supper (No. 17). By the simplest means
Bach reinforces the solemnity of the episode and by
an association of themes already pointed out (Exs. 46,
47) declares its significance. The Saviour's answer to
Judas's belated and self-accusing question (bar 15) is
accompanied on the Strings by an inversion of Ex. 46 :

Ex. 55.

Thus, simply and subtly, Bach exposes the import of
Judas's treachery.

Two reflective movements upon the precious gift
vouchsafed to the believer end the Scene. In both the
Oboi d'amore produce a sombre atmosphere, breathing
(No. 18) sighs over the Saviour's impending betrayal :

Ex. 56.

In the Aria (No. 19) it is significant that the Soul
makes her invitation to the Saviour, 'Enter in,
dear Lord, and dwell', upon the theme of consecration
already heard in No. 17 :

[1] *Op. cit.* ii. 27.

Ex. 57.
No. 17. Vn. i (bar 26).

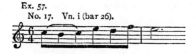

No. 19. Ob. d'am. i.

VI. THE MOUNT OF OLIVES

No. 20 (Recit.) :

St. Matthew xxvi. 30–2 (To the Mount of Olives).

No. 21 (Choral) (*as No. 3*) :

> *Regard me, then, my Saviour,*
> *My Shepherd, make me Thine.*
> *I dwell on heaven's pasture ;*
> *For Thou hast made it mine.*
> *How oft Thyself hast fed me*
> *With love for daily food ;*
> *How oft Thy spirit led me*
> *To find the Eternal Good !*

No. 22 (Recit.) :

St. Matthew xxvi. 33–5 (Peter's protestation).

No. 23 (Choral) (*as No. 16*) :

> *I too will stand beside Thee ;*
> *Lord, bid me not depart.*
> *No, never I'll desert Thee*
> *Till Thou'st endured death's smart.*

So, when Thou art o'ertaken
By death's tremendous doom,
Thou shalt not be forsaken,
But find in me Thy home.

The short Scene contains but four movements, two
Bible texts and two Chorals ; no language less con-
secrated could satisfy Bach's search for the fitting
word. No. 20, in which Christ foretells His approaching desertion by the Twelve, illustrates Bach's use of
pictorial themes. The ascent of the Mount of Olives
is represented (bar 2) by a rising passage in the Continuo :

Ex. 58.

The prophecy, 'The sheep of the flock shall be
scattered', is accompanied on the Strings by an
agitated passage *Vivace* in contrary motion between
the upper instruments and the Basses to suggest dis-
persion :

Ex. 59.

The words, 'But after I am risen again' (bar 11), are

followed by a symbolic figure of ascension, a buoyant statement of Ex. 58 :

Ex. 60.

The following Choral (No. 21), suggested by the figure of the shepherd in No. 20, is stanza v of Paul Gerhardt's 'O Haupt voll Blut und Wunden' (1656), set to an originally secular tune by Hans Leo Hassler (1601). The hymn, the principal one in the St. Matthew Passion, occurs again in Nos. 23, 53 (melody), 63, 72. It is repeated, but a semitone lower, after Peter's confident boast (No. 22). The Autograph reveals an interesting and hitherto un-observed point : Bach proposed at first to use there (No. 23) the seventh stanza, instead of the sixth, which he eventually preferred. Since No. 23 repeats the harmonic setting of No. 21, he merely added a note after No. 22 : 'Versus 2. Ich will hier bey dir stehen sequ^{tr} ex Clave Dis.' Under No. 21 he placed the same direction. In both cases the words ' Es dient zu meinen Freuden ' (the first line of stanza vii of Gerhardt's hymn) are struck out and ' Ich will ', &c., is substituted.

VII. GETHSEMANE

No. 24 (Recit.) :
St. Matthew xxvi. 36–8 (The Agony).

No. 25 (Recit. : Tenor and Choral) (2 *Fl.*, 2 *Ob.*

da caccia, Cont., and Organ ; Strings, Cont., and Organ) :

> O grief! How throbs His woe-beladen heart !
> His spirit faints! His countenance how pale !
> Now see Him swift to judgement borne ;
> No one is near, He prays forlorn.
> The pains of death are on Him falling,
> And for their prey as demons calling.
> Ah, could my loving heart but bear,
> O Lord, Thine agony and Passion,
> Give swift release and comfort fashion,
> How gladly would I share !
>
> *My Saviour, why must all this ill befall Thee ?*
> *Ah, 'tis my sin, alas, in toils hath bound Thee.*
> *'Tis I, Lord Jesus, should the pain be suffering*
> *That Thou'rt enduring.*

No. 26 (Aria : Tenor and Chorus) (*Ob., Cont., and Organ ; Strings, 2 Fl., Cont., and Organ*) :

> I'll stand beside my Jesus watching :
>> *Ch.* So shall our sins to sleep be laid.
> Snatched from hell
> By His grace, I know full well
> His Passion giveth me salvation.
>> *Ch.* Yea, 'tis His mortal tribulation
>> So bitter hath our debt all paid.

No. 27 (Recit.) :
St. Matthew xxvi. 39 (Christ's prayer).

No. 28 (Recit. : Bass) (*Strings, Cont., and Organ*) :

The Saviour bowed before His Father bendeth,
And wins for me and all creation
By His oblation
A heavenly grace that never endeth.
He ready is the cup of death's last bitterness to drain it,
In which our sins, foul poisons, lie
And to the brim with evil fill it,
For Him to drink Who's God on high.

No. 29 (Aria : Bass) (*Vn. i, ii, Cont., and Organ*) :

> Gladly will I too accept them,
> Cross and chalice, nor reject them,
> Since my dear Lord knew them too.
> For, His heart,
> With love's milk of kindness flowing,
> Hath the smart,
> How oft sorrow shall renew,
> Lightened by His earthly suffering.

No. 30 (Recit.) :

St. Matthew xxvi. 40–2 (' Thy will be done ').

No. 31 (Choral) (*as No. 3*) :

> *Whate'er God wills is best alway*
> *And ever justly founded ;*
> *E'er ready He to guide our way*
> *If faith on Him's sure grounded.*
> *For God in need*
> *Will help indeed*

II   c

And chasten but in measure.
Who trusts in God
Stands as a rod
And is deserted never.

The Agony is narrated by St. Matthew in seven
verses, distributed by Bach among three Recitatives,
annotated by five reflective movements. The expansion deliberately emphasizes the tragic significance of
the episode. In No. 24 the Saviour's 'My soul is
exceeding sorrowful' is accompanied by a throbbing
quaver rhythm which carries the sultry menace of an
approaching storm. Continued into the following
movement (No. 25), it supports the pathetic wail of
the Flutes and Oboe da caccia :

Ex. 61.

The lamentations of the Daughter of Zion are echoed
by the Faithful (No. 25) in the third stanza of Heermann's hymn, set to the tune already heard in No. 3.
Bach surrounds the melody with poignant harmonies,
and its low setting brings it to the listener as a distant
prayer. The movement, avoiding a definite close,
moves to the dominant of the key (C minor) of the
following Aria (No. 26), whose scheme, an alternation
of Solo and Chorus, is the same. But the Solo part is

more definite, and its opening theme suggests the watcher sharing the Saviour's vigil till break of dawn:

The quavers and semibreve of (*a*) sound the Watchman's call, while out of the little figure at (*b*) Bach builds up for the Chorus a crooning cradle-song appropriate to the words ' So shall our sins to sleep be laid '.

In No. 28, too, Bach was governed by a word—'The Saviour *bowed* before His Father bendeth.' The accompaniment repeats a series of short descending figures (*a*), which Bach marks *dolce*, to declare the motion one of self-surrender; introducing a single *ascending* progression (*b*) to illustrate the ' heavenly peace that never endeth ' :

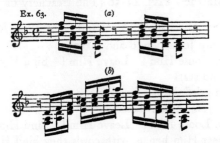

No. 29 further illustrates Bach's sensitiveness

to verbal suggestion.   Schweitzer [1] finds in it the
figure of Christ bending in agonized prayer before His
Father.   But the interpretation is contrary to the
mood of the Aria and the sense of the words, which
express the believer's eagerness to bear burdens
which the Saviour has lightened by His Cross.   The
vocal theme is suave, confident, almost cheerful,
evidently inspired by ' Gerne ' (gladly).   Not even
the word ' Cross ' attracts Bach's attention.

With No. 30 the narrative returns to the Saviour's
Agony, and the concluding Choral (No. 31) repeats
the soul's submission.   The stanza is the first of
Markgraf Albrecht of Brandenburg's ' Was mein
Gott will, das g'scheh' allzeit ' (*c.* 1554), set to a
melody of secular origin, first published at Paris in
1529.

VIII.   THE BETRAYAL

No. 32 (Recit.) :

St. Matthew xxvi. 43–50 (The treachery of Judas).

No. 33 (Duet (Sop., Alto) and Chorus) (*as No.* 1) :
Now is my Jesus bound and taken.
  Ch. Loose Him !   Leave Him !   Bind Him not !
Moon and stars
Have in grief the sky forsaken ;
For my Jesus now is taken.
  Ch. Loose Him !   Leave Him !   Bind Him not !
They bear Him hence, with cords they bind Him.

---

[1] *Op. cit.* ii. 221.

Ch. Have thunder and lightning their power for-
    gotten ?
    Then, belch forth, hell's sulphurous pit, all
      thy terrors !
    Consume them, destroy them, o'erwhelm
      them with tremors,
    With furious hand,
    The trait'rous betrayer, the murderous band !

No. 34 (Recit.) :
St. Matthew xxvi. 51–6 (The disciples forsake Jesus).

No. 35 (Choral) (*Strings, 2 Fl., 2 Ob. d'amore, Cont.,*
and Organ) :
    O man, bewail thy grievous fall,
    For which Christ left His Father's hall
    And came to earth from heaven.
    He of a maiden, virgin, pure,
    Was born, of man the Saviour sure,
    And came our ills to leaven.
    The dead He raised again to life,
    The sick He loosed from pain and strife ;
    Until the time appointed
    That He for us should shed His blood,
    And take on Him our sin's dark load,
    Stretched on the Cross accursèd.

Unlike the St. John Passion, whose Part I concludes
unarrestingly with Peter's denial, the St. Matthew
ends on an incident dramatic in itself and rendered
more so by Bach's treatment of it.

In the first of the two Recits. that unfold the

narrative (No. 32) the Saviour announces His imminent betrayal, which Bach represents as the hour of
His triumph by inserting for the last time the theme
of victory (cf. Exs. 46 and 47) :

Ex. 64.

The Saviour is now a prisoner, bound and guarded.
As in the opening Chorus, Bach pictures Him, in
No. 33, amid His captors. Above, the Flutes and
Oboes wail a theme of lamentation :

Ex. 65.

while the Strings in unison *un poco piano* give out
a syncopated subject (*a*) whose interpretation is
revealed in an Aria of the earliest version of the
St. John Passion (*b*) :

Ex. 66.
(*a*)

The phrase (*b*) interprets the word ' windet ' = twist, twine, writhe, and in No. 33 has the same meaning : it pictures the Saviour bound. An error has crept into English editions in regard to it. The Autograph distinctly directs ' Violoncelli concordant ', i. e. play the subject *in unison* with the Violins and Viola. But upon the strength of an unauthoritative manuscript —which, moreover, on examination, does not support the innovation—the Violoncelli have been permitted to play the theme an octave lower. At the words ' They bear Him hence ', a descending theme is heard from the Strings in unison, which, march-like, bears the Saviour to Calvary :

Ex. 67.

The two Choirs and Orchestras unite in the terrific outburst which forms the second part of No. 33. The thunders roar, the lightning flickers viciously in the staccato of the Flutes and Oboes, and, after the pause bar, the sudden explosion of the chord of F sharp major assails the betrayer from another quarter. Hell opens her jaws to engulf him whom the lightning has spared. The earth rocks in eruption, and nature calls for her prey. The movement is stupendous in its malignant vigour.

For that reason, perhaps, Bach felt compelled to follow No. 34, the conventional conclusion of Part I,

with another movement. In the first version of the
Passion, and, as has been shown, until the 1740's, the
first Part concluded with a simple four-part Choral.
Bach probably discarded it because it was too slight
to follow No. 33. The original opening Chorus of
the St. John Passion, ' O Mensch, bewein' dein' Sünde
gross ', on the other hand, was upon a scale and
grandeur which permitted its interpolation at this
point; while its words—stanza i of Sebald Heyden's
hymn (1525)—sound a personal challenge to the
hearer to find within himself the betrayer of his
Master. The melody is Matthäus Greitter's (1525).
The semiquaver figure on the Flutes and Oboes is one
of Bach's characteristic motives of lamentation :

Ex. 68. Fl. i, ii.

But the whole movement is charged with emotion,
and in craftsmanship is not excelled by any of the
great Choral Fantasias in the Cantatas of Bach's
maturest period.

PART II

IX. PROLOGUE

No. 36 (Aria (Alto) and Chorus) (*Strings, Fl. i, Ob.
d'am. i, Cont., and Organ ; Strings, Cont., and Organ*) :
Grief ! now is my Jesus gone.

Ch. Where is then thy Friend hence departed,
    O thou fairest of mortal women?
Nay I know not nor can show ye.

Ch. Where hath now thy Friend from thee strayed?
Ah, my Lamb, fierce tigers claw Thee!
Grief! where is my Jesus gone?

Ch. We would go forth with thee to seek Him.
Howe'er shall my fond heart make answer
When she asks, Where is my Master?
Grief! where is my Jesus gone?

After the deep sincerity of No. 35, the opening of
Part II is somewhat artificial : Picander is too evident.
Zion and the Faithful vainly seek the Saviour, Zion
herself flitting hither and thither on restless vocal
roulades whose lowest notes build up a chromatic
grief motive :

Ex. 69.
Fl., Ob., Vn. i.

In the second part of the Aria, the *coloratura* on the
word ' klauen ' appears, with three vicious stabs, to
represent the beast's assault :

Ex. 70.

X. CHRIST BEFORE CAIAPHAS

No. 37 (Recit.) :

St. Matthew xxvi. 57–60 (The priests seek false
witness).

No. 38 (Choral) (*as No. 3*) :
> *How false the world its part doth play,*
> *What lies and evil thoughts doth say,*
> *So eager to condemn me !*
> *Lord, in my need*
> *For help I plead ;*
> *From lying tongues protect me !*

No. 39 (Recit.) :
St. Matthew xxvi. 60–3 (The false witnesses).

No. 40 (Recit. : Tenor) (*2 Ob., Cont., and Organ*) :
No word He speaks, my Lord, false witness scorning,
And so thereby would teach us
That He, with pity for us burning,
E'en death's last sorrow will endure ;
O let us too, when troubles fall,
Like Him go meet them all,
In silent faith affliction bearing.

No. 41 (Aria : Tenor) (*Vcello and Organ*) :
> Endure, faint heart !
> Though men falsely rail against me,
> Still I'll show the braver part,
> Bear the rod ;
> For I know my dearest Lord
> Holds me guiltless, will avenge me.

Nos. 42–5 (Recits. and Choruses):
St. Matthew xxvi. 63–8 (Christ is buffeted).

No. 46 (Choral) (*as No. 3*):
Who dareth, Lord, to smite Thee,
And falsely here indict Thee,
Misjudge and wound Thee so?
Of sin Thy soul is guiltless;
'Tis we and ours are witness
Of sin's long tale of ill and woe.

The drama reopens in the hall of Caiaphas, which
the scribes, priests, and elders fill with accusation of
the Saviour, seeking evidence for his condemnation.
The Choral (No. 38) is not happily chosen; it diverts
attention from the Sinless to the sinner, whom it
also represents as the innocent victim of rancour.
The words are the fifth stanza of Adam Reissner's ' In
dich hab' ich gehoffet, Herr ' (1533), set to Seth
Calvisius's melody (1581).

In No. 39 the false witnesses appear. By a characteristic stroke of realism Bach makes them sing the
same notes in canon, to expose their false story as
pre-concocted:

Ex. 71.

In No. 40 the detached quaver chords in the accompaniment measure the Saviour's silence before His

accusers with the regularity of a chronometer. In the
following Aria (No. 41), too, His patient reticence is
expressed in the Violoncello *obbligato*, where a suave
subject alternates throughout with a restless rhythm
which represents the 'false tongues' of the accusers :

Ex. 72.

Questioned by the High Priest (No. 42), the Saviour
declares His Godhead : 'Hereafter shall ye see the
Son of Man sitting on the right hand of power.'
In the accompaniment Bach paints the clouds of
glory :

Ex. 73.

The dramatic Chorus (No. 43) effectively represents
the malevolence of the Saviour's enemies. In the
space of two bars each of the eight vocal parts (and
with them Flutes, Oboes, and Strings) enters separately
upon a phrase so built that the emphasis is always on
the word 'schuldig' (guilty) :

Ex. 74.

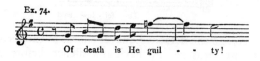

Of   death   is He   guil - - ty!

A similar impression of multitudinous clamour is created by the antiphony of the mocking Chorus (No. 45), ' Now tell us '. The full Orchestra (as in No. 1) is employed in these derisory Choruses, in which the Flutes alone have independent parts, which, written high, accentuate the mockery.

The scene ends (No. 46) with stanza iii of Gerhardt's hymn, to the melody already heard in No. 16. Bach marks it ' Stromenti concordant ' in the Score, the only Choral so distinguished, and for a reason not apparent.

XI. PETER'S DENIAL

Nos. 47–8 (Recits. and Chorus) :

St. Matthew xxvi. 69–end (Peter denies Christ).

No. 48 (Aria : Alto) (*Vn. Solo, Strings, Cont., and Organ*) :

> Have mercy, Lord, my God,
> Regard my piteous crying !
> See'st Thou not eyes are heavy,
> Weep for Thee bitterly ?
> Have mercy, Lord !

No. 49 (Choral) (*as No. 3*) :

> *Once in sin from Thee I parted,*
> *Now I seek Thy face again ;*
> *For Thy Son, so loving-hearted,*
> *Grace hath won me through His pain.*
> *Nought of mine the debt can pay,*
> *But God's love can sin outweigh ;*
> *Strong and sure it fails us never,*
> *Mine it is and shall be ever.*

The Scene turns to Peter, the story of whose moral collapse breaks in upon the principal tragedy. Thrice (No. 47) he is challenged to confess his discipleship, each time in tones subtly differentiated by Bach. First, a maidservant, conversational, almost indifferent:

Ex. 75.

Now wast thou not al - so with Je - sus of Ga - li - lae - a?

Peter next overhears the whispered statement of another maid. Her phrase is on a downward curve and positive :

Ex. 76.

This man al - so was with Je - sus of Na - za - reth

The third time bystanders put the question directly. Its tone is not unfriendly, but emphatic and convinced. Only once the voices sing 'surely'. But the Continuo repeats the word in every bar :

Ex. 77.

[Sure-ly,   sure-ly,   sure-ly,   sure-ly]

while the busy Flutes above seem to speak for the chattering maids.

Bach's setting of the last eight bars of No. 48 (Recit.) may be compared with his earlier treatment of them in the St. John Passion (No. 18). The crowing of the cock is much more realistic, but the melisma on ' wept bitterly ' is much less exaggerated. With a touch of realism, too, Peter's last denial is sung to a passionate phrase which the Evangelist immediately echoes to record the prophecy of Peter's downfall fulfilled :

Ex. 78.

I   know not the man.   And im - me - diately the cock crew

The simplicity of the melisma in the Recit. (No. 48) is accounted for by the fact that it is prolonged into the following Aria (No. 48), so that the weeping of the repentant disciple accompanies the singer's petition. It is not merely a coincidence that the first notes of the Aria repeat Peter's phrase of denial. The penitent receives a message of comfort in the Choral (No. 49), in which the sixth stanza of Johann Rist's ' Werde munter, mein Gemüthe ' (1642) is set to Johann Schop's melody (1642). The Tenor part especially breathes divine grace.

XII. THE END OF JUDAS

Nos. 50–1 (Recits. and Chorus) :

St. Matthew xxvii. 1–6 (Judas hangs himself).

No. 51 (Aria : Bass) (*Vn. Solo, Strings, Cont., and Organ*) :

> Quickly, Christ my Lord restore me !
> See the price of blood, the gold
> At your feet in pieces rolled
> By the traitor guilty !

The short Scene introduces another (No. 50) of the concise dramatic Choruses which distinguish the St. Matthew from the earlier Passion ; they are of exceptional length if they number ten bars. No. 50, in which both Choirs and Orchestras (as No. 1) are employed, has only five, but they suffice to portray the bland formalism of official utterance.

The words of the Aria (No. 51) are addressed to the priests, whose repulsion of Judas leaves the Saviour still in bonds. The music seems ill fitted to the words, with its bright tonality (G major) and the striking curves of the Violin *obbligato* :

Ex. 79.

whose widely dispersed notes picture Judas, with a sweeping gesture, flinging down the twenty pieces.

XIII. CHRIST BEFORE PILATE

No. 52 (Recit.) :

St. Matthew xxvii. 7–14 (Christ examined by Pilate),

No. 53 (Choral) (*as No. 3*) :
> *On Jesus lay thy sorrow,*
> *Thy burden and thy cares.*
> *There dawns a bright to-morrow*
> *That mourning wrings from tears.*
> *For He the heavens that rideth,*
> *And speeds the winds in flight,*
> *Thy ways also provideth*
> *And leadeth thee aright.*

No. 54 (Recit. and Choruses) :
St. Matthew xxvii. 15–22 (Pilate looseth Barabbas).

No. 55 (Choral) (*as No. 3*) :
> *O wondrous love such punishment endureth!*
> *The faithful Shepherd for His flock life giveth,*
> *The Master pays the debt by servants owing,*
> *Their fault excusing!*

No. 56 (Recit.) :
St. Matthew xxvii. 23 ('What evil hath He done?').

No. 57 (Recit. : Soprano) (2 *Ob. da caccia, Cont., and Organ*) :
> To all men Jesus good hath done :
> The blind man hath received his sight,
> The man born lame now walketh.
> God's holy Word He hath us taught,
> For us the devil fought.
> The mourner hath He comforted,
> The sinner takes He by the hand.
> Than good Lord Jesus naught hath planned.

II D

No. 58 (Aria : Soprano) (1 *Fl.*, 2 *Ob. da caccia*) :
> For love of man the Saviour dieth,
> Who knoweth naught of shame and sin.
> Thus my soul damnation flieth,
> Nor shall hell my body win,
> Not as victim claim my spirit.

Nos. 59–60 (Recits. and Choruses) :
St. Matthew xxvii. 23–6 (Jesus is scourged).

No. 61 (Recit. : Alto) (*Strings, Cont., and Organ*) :
> Have pity, God !
> Here stands the Saviour bound and wounded,
> By torturers to death is hounded !
> Tormentors, stay your hand !
> Are not your hearts to pity moved
> At sight of anguish patient borne ?
> Alas ! Your hearts are cold,
> And must be hard as rock itself,
> Yea, sterner, harder, still.
> Have pity ! Stay your hand !

No. 61 (Aria : Alto) (*Vn. i, ii (unis.), Cont., and Organ*) :
> Can my tears not move Thy pity ?
> Fall they vainly ?
> Look within my heart and see !
> Yea, and let it—hear my pleading !—
> When the Saviour's wounds are bleeding
> As a chalice neath them be.

No. 62 (Recit. and Chorus) :

St. Matthew xxvii. 27–30 (Jesus is mocked).

No. 63 (Choral) (*as No.* 3) :

> *O sacred Head, encircled*
> *With crown of piercing thorn !*
> *O bleeding Head, empurpled,*
> *Reviled, insulted, torn,*
> *Thou once in highest glory*
> *Wast throned mid songs and praise,*
> *But now art bent before me ;*
> *To Thee my soul I raise.*
>
> *O Countenance Almighty,*
> *Before Whom bent in awe*
> *The universe so mighty*
> *And took from Thee its law ;*
> *How pale and wan Thy features,*
> *How dim Thy drooping gaze !*
> *Who is't of Thine own creatures*
> *Mad insult to Thee pays ?*

As the tragedy moves to its climax the closer is it annotated with reflective movements. The present Section is punctuated by three Chorals and two Arioso Recits., each with a dependent Aria. Of the Chorals, No. 53 is the first stanza of Paul Gerhardt's 'Befiehl du deine Wege' (1656), to the melody already heard in No. 21 ; No. 55 is the fourth stanza, to the same melody, of Heermann's hymn already heard in No. 3 ; No. 64 sets stanzas i and ii of Gerhardt's hymn, 'O Haupt voll Blut' (see No. 21). All the Choruses in the section are for both Choirs and Orchestras (as in No. 1).

Pilate, eager to release one whose offence he cannot recognize, seeks (No. 52) escape from a dilemma by exercising his power of reprieve. The Jews prefer Barabbas in a mighty shout (No. 54), after the manner of the older Passions. Bach's inclination to brevity here was influenced by the fact that, unlike the St. John Passion, no lyrical movement interrupts between the 'Barabbas' and the 'Crucify', impeding the rapid unfolding of the drama. With significance, as has been pointed out already, the two Choirs and Orchestras unite in the short Chorus (No. 54), 'Crucify', in which the 'Cross' motive is prominent:

Ex. 80.

Cru - ci - fy, cru - ci - fy . . . . . .

Unlike the equivalent movement in the St. John Passion, the mood of the Chorus is resolute rather than fanatical.

Nos. 57 and 58 interrupt the action. But Pilate's question, 'What evil hath He done?' (No. 56), afforded Picander an opening which he was unable to resist. A Soprano voice answers Pilate's question in a Recitative (No. 57), whose sombre accompaniment and syncopated rhythm contrast the stricken Saviour with His good deeds of which the voice sings:

Ex. 81.
Ob. da caccia.

The following Aria (No. 58), in A minor, also replies to Pilate's question. It extols the Saviour's love, and throughout is informed by that word ('Liebe'). Lacking a Bass foundation,[1] it seems to 'hover in the air', where the Flute weaves a melody which falls to earth like a lark's song :

Ex. 82.

The narrative is resumed (No. 59). Again the shout, 'Crucify', is raised, this time a tone higher than before, as if to mark the growing tensity. Pilate surrenders to the clamour but disowns responsibility. The crowd, still unanimous (Choir I and II in unison), lightly assumes it : 'His blood be upon us and on our children.' The steady Continuo supports the confident words :

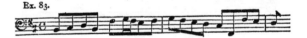

Ex. 83.

No. 60 affords another comparison between this and Bach's earlier setting of the Passion story. In the St. John (No. 30) he inserts an excessive melisma on the word 'scourged', which almost pain-

[1] The Autograph Score expressly directs 'senza Organo'.

fully represents the strokes falling on the Saviour's
flesh.   Here the word passes without emphasis.   The
reason may be found in the fact that, as in the passage
recording Peter's remorse, Picander provided Bach
with a separate movement in which to elaborate the
episode.   In the Recit. (No. 60) that follows, a
rhythmical figure on the Strings represents the falling
scourge :

Ex. 84.

It is continued (*a*) into the following Aria (No. 61),
where another theme (*b*) is added which, transferred to
the vocal part, portrays the agony of the soul witnessing
the Redeemer's torture, and ends with a cry that is
almost a shriek of despair :

Ex. 85.

Vn. i, ii.   (*a*)

Handel uses the identical rhythm in the same context
in the *Messiah* (No. 23) :

Ex. 86.

He gave His back to the smi-ters

The concise Chorus (No. 62), ' All hail ', is much shorter than the corresponding movement (No. 34) of the St. John Passion, and lacks its pictorial illustration. As in No. 45 the Chorus is antiphonal. Stanzas i and ii of Gerhardt's Passion hymn appropriately bring the Section, so charged with tragedy, to an end (No. 63).

XIV. CALVARY

No. 64 (Recit.) :

St. Matthew xxvii. 31–2 (Simon bears the Cross).

No. 65 (Recit. : Bass) (2 *Fl.*, *Va. da gamba*, *Cont.*, *and Organ*) :

How gladly would we that our flesh and blood
To sin were crucified ;
The better for our spirit's good,
The more we'd death abide.

No. 66 (Aria : Bass) (*Va. da gamba*, *Cont.*, *and Organ*) :

Come, kindly Cross, I'd fain embrace thee !
My Jesus, let myself it bear !
And if its burden be too sore,
Then help my weakness, I implore Thee.

Nos. 67–8 (Recits. and Choruses) :
St. Matthew xxvii. 33–44 (The Crucifixion).

No. 69 (Recit. : Alto) (2 *Ob. da caccia, Vcello, Cont.,
and Organ*) :
Ah, Golgotha, unkindly Golgotha !
The Lord of earth and heaven must on thee shameful
    perish.
The blessed Saviour of our race
Upon the Cross now bows His face ;
The God Who heaven and earth created
To death and agony is fated.
The Sinless here as sinners dieth.
My soul 's in grief and dark despair.
Ah Golgotha, unkindly Golgotha !

No. 70 (Aria (Alto) and Chorus) (2 *Ob. da caccia,
Cont., and Organ ; Strings, 2 Ob., Cont., and Organ*) :
Hither ! Jesus' outstretched arm
Calls us now to peace and calm.
Come !
        Ch. Come where ?
On Jesu's bosom find salvation,
Consolation.
Seek it !
        Ch. Where ?
On Jesu's bosom.
Living, dying,
Rest ye there,
All ye sick and lost ones here !
Rest ye !

Ch. Where ?
On Jesu's bosom.

St. Matthew adds a circumstance not mentioned by
St. John—Simon of Cyrene's enforced bearing of the
Cross to Calvary (No. 64). Picander interpolates two
reflective movements in which the worshipper declares
his readiness also to bear the Cross. In No. 65 the
Flutes, in broken phrases, portray the Saviour moving
along the path of sacrifice :

Ex. 87.

The Aria (No. 66) repeats the picture sketched in
the preceding Recit. Schweitzer [1] sees Simon striding
confidently where the Saviour had walked painfully.
But the panting rhythm of the Viola da gamba and
its exaggerated intervals convey an impression not
merely of stumbling but of actual falling :

Ex. 88.

The march-like Continuo also, which Bach marks
p. e staccato, is broken up in a manner that rejects
Schweitzer's interpretation : clearly it represents toil-
some ascent of the hill of doom :

Ex. 89.

[1] *Op. cit.* ii. 230.

In Kirnberger's copy of the Score the Gamba *obbligato*
is given to the Lute, an instrument whose use was in
decline in the eighteenth century, though Bach wrote
a Partita for it.

The two Choruses (No. 67) sung beneath the Cross
differ from the other utterances of the Jews in the
Score. St. John records neither outburst, ' Thou that
destroy'st the Temple of God,' nor ' He saved others,
Himself He cannot save'. Bach contributes to both
a tone of passionate fanaticism characteristic of the
Choruses in the St. John, but absent elsewhere in the
St. Matthew. Both employ the resources of both
Choirs and Orchestras (as No. 1). In the first, very
arresting is the emphatic and derisory ' Save Thyself '
hurled at the passive Saviour by the eight voices
separately over four bars, and the mocking invitation,
on a descending phrase :

Ex. 90.

Come down, ... come down . . . .

repeated in the second Chorus :

Ex. 91.

Come down,   come down, come down   from   the   Cross!

Both Choruses, like their predecessors, begin anti-
phonally. But the crowds unite in their venom, and
the second Chorus ends—the only instance in the
work—on a choral unison.

The crowd disperses. The Sufferer hangs aloft on

the Cross while Zion sings her lament (No. 69), 'Ah, Golgotha!' The Oboe da caccia give it mournful colour, while below, in Bach's invariable idiom, the Violoncelli *pizzicato* toll the funeral bells:

Ex. 92.

In the Aria (No. 70) the orchestral colour of No. 69 is repeated, but the mourning bells are silent. Zion summons the faithful to shelter within the Saviour's arms outstretched upon the Cross. The Continuo is shaped throughout to space their wide embrace:

Ex. 93.

The interjected questions of the Chorus are a feature Bach already had used in the St. John Passion (No. 48). Like Picander, he found his model in Brockes's text.

XV. THE NINTH HOUR

No. 71 (Recit. and Choruses):
St. Matthew xxvii. 45–50 (The end).

No. 72 (Choral) (*as No. 3*):
    When life's last hour shall call me,
    Be present at my side ;
    Let no dread fears appal me ;
    Thy mercy, Lord, is wide.

And when my heart must languish
Prepare the path I go,
And let Thy Cross and anguish
Assuage my deepest woe.

No. 73 (Recits. and Chorus) :

St. Matthew xxvii. 51–8 (The Earthquake ; Joseph of Arimathaea).

No. 74 (Recit. : Bass) (*Strings, Cont., and Organ*) :
At even, hour of calm and rest,
Was Adam's sin made manifest.
At eventide 'twas Christ for sin atonèd.
At even, too, the dove returnèd,
An olive leaf of promise bearing.
O beauteous hour, God's love declaring !
Now God with man is reconciled in peace ;
For Jesus hath endured the Cross.
His body sinks to rest.
Go, loving servant, make thy quest !
Go, gently bear the Saviour's lifeless body,
A precious load, a burden fair and holy !

No. 75 (Aria : Bass) (*Strings, 2 Ob. da caccia, Cont., and Organ*) :
Purge thyself, my heart, of sin,
So shall Jesus rest within thee.
Let Him there, while life shall last,
Take His rest
Evermore, at peace so calmly.
World, depart !   Come, Jesus, in !

The opening Recit. (No. 71) illustrates Bach's attention to his text and the closeness with which he visualized its scenes. St. Matthew and St. Mark record the words, ' Eli, Eli, lama sabachthani ? ', as the last the Saviour spoke, the outcry of His humanity. Bach therefore withdraws, for the only time, the halo which shines elsewhere upon His every utterance : the accompanying Strings are silent, the Organ takes their place. Soft, sustained notes support His words, displacing the detached crotchet chords which accompany the other Bible Recitatives.

The Choruses (No. 71), ' He calleth for Elias ', and ' Wait, let us see ', short, direct, are assigned to the two Choirs in turn. A dramatic effect is created by this division of the bystanders into two bodies. It is significant, too, that the Flutes are silent in the first, while in the second Chorus their eager semiquavers add a detail of mockery consonant with the words. For the last time, and impressively (No. 72), Gerhardt's hymn (stanza ix) is sung to its accustomed melody.

Bach had already in the St. John Passion (No. 61) set St. Matthew's description of the earthquake. Its representation here is more violent, but a comparison of the two movements shows how consistent Bach is in the curve and inflexion of his phrases. With doubtful judgement, and contrary to Bach's intention, Mendelssohn orchestrated the accompaniment for the revival performance of the Passion at Leipzig in 1829.

Only St. Matthew among the Evangelists puts the admission, ' Truly this was the son of God ' (No. 73) into the mouth of the centurion *and others*. So Bach unites both Choirs and Orchestras in this act of reluctant homage, and, significantly, the mocking Flutes are silent.

The two reflective movements that follow bring the Section to a very peaceful and tender conclusion. In the first (No. 74), above an unfigured Pedal-point, the Violins *sempre p.* breathe a tranquil subject which seems, as Spitta [1] comments, to gather the tender mists of twilight :

Ex. 94.

A similar ineffable sense of calm pervades the Aria (No. 75). 'World, depart; come, Jesus, in ! ' sings the voice, declaring a joy that is now calm, now exuberant, always chastened ; for constantly the Oboes repeat the rhythm of lamentation already observed in No. 35 (Ex. 68).

XVI. THE BURIAL

No. 76 (Recits. and Chorus) :
St. Matthew xxvii. 59–end (Christ's burial).

No. 77 (Recit. (S. A. T. B.) and Chorus) *(Strings, Cont., and Organ ; Strings, 2 Fl., 2 Ob., Cont., and Organ)* :
So now the Lord in peace doth dwell.
    Ch. Lord Jesus, fare Thee well !
His toil is o'er for our offences on Him fell.

[1] *Op. cit.* ii. 560.

Ch. Lord Jesus, fare Thee well !
Poor body, spent and holy,
See, with repentant tear-drops I bedew Thee
Whom 'tis my sin hath brought to such a plight !
    Ch. Lord Jesus, fare Thee well !
Now all my life, O Lord, I'll give Thee thanks and
    love,
Who through Thy Passion draw'st my soul above.
    Ch. Lord Jesus, fare Thee well !

No. 78 (Chorus) (*as No.* 1) :

    Here, laid to rest, in tears we leave Thee
    So calm within earth's quiet deep.
    Rest Thou softly, gently sleep !
    Rest Thy members worn and weary,
    Rest Thou softly, gently sleep !
    From Thy grave shall love divine
    Cheer the mourner, sad and weeping,
    Bring the weary to Thy keeping
    Where the soul for rest doth pine.
    Rest Thou softly, softly sleep !
    Dearest Lord,
    Slumber on, O Saviour mine !

St. John's Gospel provides no Bible Chorus after the
soldiers' disputation over the Saviour's vesture.
St. Matthew records a last interview of the priests
with Pilate. There is studied formality in their
address (No. 76), 'Sir, we remember that that deceiver
said '. But the words of the Saviour's ' blasphemy '
unite the two Choirs in a common recollection of the

prophecy of His resurrection, repeating fugally an
appropriately ascending phrase :

Ex. 95.

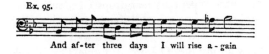

And af-ter three days   I will rise a - gain

At the evening hour Zion's faithful gather at the
grave, and the words of farewell are spoken. Beautiful
and tender as is the movement (No. 77), Picander, in
writing the words, had in mind the funeral ceremony
customary at Leipzig, where tributes to the departed
were offered by relations and others. Here each voice
in turn throws a blossom of remembrance into the
tomb, and Zion, last of all, repeats the conventional
formula, ' Habt lebenslang vor euer Leiden tausend
Dank.'

Like the St. John Passion, Bach chooses a dance
rhythm for the final Chorus (No. 78). Its original is
a Sarabande,[1] whose composition must date from the
Cöthen period : [2]

Ex. 96.

[1] *B. G.* xlv (1), p. 164.
[2] The words also are an adaptation by Picander of his 1725
text.

In more than one place the words fit the music awkwardly. The resemblances between the movement and No. 67 of the St. John have been pointed out.[1] In both the Saviour's body sinks into the grave on descending phrases closely similar. The music moves with the rhythm of a funeral march. But over it floats an atmosphere of serenest peace and calm—

Slumber on, O Saviour mine!

[1] *Supra*, p. 5.

II   E

IV. *The St. Mark Passion*

(1731)

In addition to those already considered, Picander
wrote [1] a third 'Texte zur Passions-Music nach dem
Evangelisten Marco am Char-Freytage 1731'. Entirely
upon the lines of the St. Matthew Passion, written
three years earlier, it is in two Parts ('Vor der Predigt',
'Nach der Predigt'), adopts the literal Bible text
(chaps. xiv and xv), and, though less plentifully, is
supplied with original stanzas—opening and closing
Chorus and six Arias—and a very liberal provision of
Chorals (eight in each Part). The work certainly was
performed in St. Thomas's on Good Friday, 1731.
The Score, no longer extant, was in existence in 1764 :
it is referred to in Breitkopf's New Year Catalogue :
'*Anonymo*. Passions-Cantate, *secundum Marcum*. Geh,
Jesu, geh zu deiner Pein.' Bach's authorship, however, can be asserted positively ; five of its eight
lyrical numbers are identified with movements in the
Trauer-Ode composed in 1727 in commemoration of
the Electress-Queen Christiane Eberhardine, a dis-
covery made by Wilhelm Rust.[2]

Therefore it can be assumed that the remaining
Arias also are borrowed. From what source ? It was
not Bach's habit to lock up music that could be used

---

[1] Published in Part III of his 'Gedichte', pp. 44–61.
[2] *B. G.* xx (2), p. viii.

on other occasions. About 1730—certainly subsequent to February 1728—he wrote for his wife a Chamber Cantata, ' Ich bin in mir vergnügt ', whose first Aria is built upon a stanza metrically identical with that of No. 19 *infra* : the ' Ist der ' of the second lines of both also cannot be overlooked. Judged by Bach's practice elsewhere there is no difficulty in accepting the music of the Cantata Aria as that which he borrowed for the St. Mark Passion. Moreover, there is a close metrical resemblance between No. 34 *infra* and No. 8 of the same Cantata. Their stanzas do not conform exactly, but the music of the Cantata Aria is easily adaptable. There remains Aria No. 42 *infra*. Its metrical structure is quite abnormal; only one other exactly similar to it is found among Bach's Cantatas, the Bass Solo (No. 2) of Cantata 7. The work, however, dates from a period subsequent to 1731.

The following is Picander's libretto. Bach's ascertained or conjectured association with it is indicated.

Vor der Predigt

No. 1[1] (Chorus) :

Geh, Jesu, geh zu deiner Pein !
Ich will so lange dich beweinen,
Bis mir dein Trost wird wieder scheinen,
Da ich versöhnet werde sein.

[No. 1 of the *Trauer-Ode* :

Lass, Fürstin, lass noch einen Strahl
Aus Salems Sterngewölben schiessen,
Und sieh, mit wieviel Thränengüssen
Umringen wir dein Ehrenmahl.]

[1] The movements are unnumbered in the libretto.

E 2

No. 2 (Recits. and Choruses) :
St. Mark xiv. 1–5 (Christ's head is anointed).

No. 3 (Choral) :

> *Sie stellen uns wie Ketzern nach,* &c.

>> (St. iv of Justus Jonas's 'Wo Gott der Herr
>> nicht bei uns hält' (1524).)
>> [As a Tenor Unison Choral in Cantata 178, No. 4.
>> Simple four-part harmony *ibid.*, No. 7.]

No. 4 (Recits.) :
St. Mark xiv. 6–11 (Judas sells his Master).

No. 5 (Choral) :

> *Mir hat die Welt trüglich gericht,* &c.

>> (St. v of Adam Reissner's 'In dich hab' ich
>> gehoffet, Herr' (1533).)
>> [St. Matthew Passion, No. 38.]

No. 6 (Recits. and Chorus) :
St. Mark xiv. 12–19 (Christ foretells His betrayal).

No. 7 (Choral) :

> *Ich, ich und meine Sünden,* &c.

>> (St. iv of Paul Gerhardt's 'O Welt, sieh' hier
>> dein Leben' (1647).)
>> [St. John Passion, No. 15.]

No. 8 (Recits.) :
St. Mark xiv. 20–5 (Institution of the Holy Supper).

No. 9 (Aria) :

> Mein Heiland, dich vergess ich nicht,
> Ich habe dich in mich verschlossen,

Und deinen Leib und Blut genossen,
Und meinen Trost auf dich gericht.

[No. 5 of the *Trauer-Ode* :
Wie starb die Heldin so vergnügt !
Wie muthig hat ihr Geist gerungen,
Da sie des Todes Arm bezwungen,
Noch eh' er ihre Brust besiegt !]

No. 10 (Recits.) :
St. Mark xiv. 26–8 (' All ye shall be offended ').

No. 11 (Choral) :
Wach auf, O Mensch, vom Sünden-Schlaf, &c.

> (St. xiii of Johann Rist's ' O Ewigkeit, du
> Donnerwort ' (1642).)
> [Cf. Cantatas 20 and 60.]

No. 12 (Recits.) :
St. Mark xiv. 29–34 (The Agony).

No. 13 (Choral) :
Betrübtes Herz, sei wohlgemuth, &c.

> (St. i of Andreas Kritzelmann's hymn (1627).)

No. 14 (Recits.) :
St. Mark xiv. 35–6 (' Not what I will '.)

No. 15 (Choral) :
Machs mit mir, Gott, nach deiner Güt, &c.

> (St. i of Joh. H. Schein's hymn (1628).   Cf. St. John
> Passion, No. 40.)

No. 16 (Recits.) :
St. Mark xiv. 37–42 (The betrayer is at hand).

No. 17 (Aria) :
 Er kommt, er kommt, er ist vorhanden !
 Mein Jesu, ach ! er suchet dich,
 Entfliehe doch, und lasse mich,
 Mein Heil, statt deiner in den Banden.

[No. 3 of the *Trauer-Ode* :
 Verstummt, verstummt, ihr holden Saiten !
 Kein Ton vermag der Länder Noth
 Bei ihrer theuren Mutter Tod —
 O Schmerzenswort ! — recht anzudeuten.]

No. 18 (Recits.) :
St. Mark xiv. 43–5 (The kiss of Judas).

No. 19 (Aria) :
 Falsche Welt, dein schmeichelnd Küssen
 Ist der Frommen Seelen-Gift.
 Deine Zungen sind voll Stechen,
 Und die Worte, die sie sprechen,
 Sind zu Fallen angestifft.

[? ' Ich bin in mir vergnügt ', No. 2 :
 Ruhig und in sich zufrieden
 Ist der grösste Schatz der Welt.
 Nichts geniesset, der geniesset,
 Was der Erdenkreis umschliesset,
 Der ein armes Herz behält.]

No. 20 (Recits.) :
St. Mark xiv. 46–9 (Jesus is taken).

No. 21 (Choral) :

Jesu, ohne Missethat im Garten fürhanden, &c.

(St. viii of Paul Stockmann's ' Jesu Leiden,
Pein und Tod ' (1633).)
[Cf. St. John Passion, Nos. 20, 56, 60.]

No. 22 (Recit.) :

St. Mark xiv. 50–2 (They all forsake Him).

No. 23 (Choral) :

Ich will hier bei dir stehen, &c.

(St. vi of Paul Gerhardt's ' O Haupt voll Blut
und Wunden ' (1656).)
[St. Matthew Passion, No. 23.]

Nach der Predigt

No. 24 (Aria):

Mein Tröster ist nicht mehr bei mir.

Mein Jesu, soll ich dich verlieren,

Und zum Verderben sehen führen ?

Das kömmt der Seele schmerzlich für.

Der Unschuld, welche nichts verbrochen,

Dem Lamm, das ohne Missethat,

Wird in dem ungerechten Rath

Ein Todes-Urtheil zugesprochen.

[No. 8 of the *Trauer-Ode* :

Der Ewigkeit saphirnes Haus

Zieht, Fürstin, deine heitern Blicke

Von unsrer Niedrigkeit zurücke,

Und tilgt der Erden Denkbild aus.

Ein starker Glanz von hundert Sonnen,

Der unsern Tag zur Mitternacht

Und unsre Sonne finster macht,

Hat dein verklärtes Haupt umsponnen.]

No. 25 (Recits.) :
St. Mark xiv. 53–9 (The false witnesses).

No. 26 (Choral) :

Was Menschen-Kraft und Witz anfäht, &c.

(St. ii of Justus Jonas's hymn.)
[As a Recit. and Choral in Cantata 178, No. 2. Cf.
No. 3 *supra*.]

No. 27 (Recits.) :
St. Mark xiv. 60–1 (Christ is silent before Pilate).

No. 28 (Choral) :

Befiehl du deine Wege, &c.

(St. i of Paul Gerhardt's hymn (1656).)
[St. Matthew Passion, No. 53.]

No. 29 (Recits. and Chorus) :
St. Mark xiv. 61–5 (Christ is buffeted).

No. 30 (Choral) :

Du edles Angesichte, &c.

(St. ii of Paul Gerhardt's ' O Haupt voll Blut
und Wunden ' (1656).)
[St. Matthew Passion, No. 63.]

No. 31 (Recits. and Chorus) :
St. Mark xiv. 66–end (Peter denieth Christ).

No. 32 (Choral) :

Herr, ich habe missgehandelt, &c.

(St. i of Johann Franck's hymn (1653). See
' 'Bach's Four-part Chorals ', Nos. 140–1.)

No. 33 (Recits. and Choruses) :
St. Mark xv. 1–14 (' Crucify Him ').

No. 34 (Aria) :

    Angenehmes Mord-Geschrei !
    Jesus soll am Creuze sterben,
    Nur damit ich vom Verderben
    Der verdammten Seelen frei,
    Und damit mir Creuz und Leiden
    Sanffte zu ertragen sei.

[? ' Ich bin in mir vergnügt ', No. 8 :

    Himmlische Vergnügsamkeit !
    Welches Herz sich dir ergiebet,
    Lebet allzeit unbetrübet
    Und geniesst der goldnen Zeit.]

No. 35 (Recits. and Chorus) :
St. Mark xv. 15–19 (He is crowned with thorns).

No. 36 (Choral) :
    Man hat dich sehr hart verhöhnet, &c.

        (St. iv of Ernst Chr. Homburg's ' Jesu, meines
           Lebens Leben ' (1659).)

No. 37 (Recit.) :
St. Mark xv. 20–4 (The Crucifixion).

No. 38 (Choral) :
    Das Wort sie sollen lassen stahn, &c.

        (St. iv of Luther's ' Ein feste Burg ist unser
           Gott ' (1529).)
        [Cantata 80, No. 8.]

No. 39 (Recits. and Choruses) :
St. Mark xv. 25–34 (' Why hast Thou forsaken
Me ? ').

No. 40 (Choral) :

> *Keinen hat Gott verlassen,* &c.

>> (St. i of Andreas Kessler's (?) hymn (1611).
>> See 'Bach's Four-part Chorals', No. 223.)

No. 41 (Recits. and Chorus) :
St. Mark xv. 35–7 (The End).

No. 42 (Aria) :

> Welt und Himmel, nehmt zu Ohren,
> Jesus schreiet überlaut.
> Allen Sündern sagt er an,
> Dass er nun genug gethan,
> Dass das Eden aufgebaut,
> Welches wir zuvor verloren.

No. 43 (Recits.) :
St. Mark xv. 38–45 (Joseph asks for the body of Jesus).

No. 44 (Choral) :

> *O Jesu du, Mein Hilf und Ruh !* &c.

>> (St. viii of Johann Rist's ' O Traurigkeit, O
>> Herzeleid' (1641). See 'Bach's Four-part
>> Chorals', No. 299.)

No. 45 (Recit.) :
St. Mark xv. 46–end (The Burial).

No. 46 (Chorus) :

> Bei deinem Grab und Leichen-Stein
> Will ich mich stets, mein Jesu, weiden,
> Und über dein verdienstlich Leiden
> Von Herzen froh und dankbar sein.

Schau, diese Grabschrift sollst du haben :
Mein Leben kommt aus deinem Tod,
Hier hab ich meine Sünden-Noth
Und Jesum selbst in mich begraben.

[No. 10 of the *Trauer-Ode* :

Doch, Königin ! du stirbest nicht,
Man weiss, was man an dir besessen ;
Die Nachwelt wird dich nicht vergessen,
Bis dieser Weltbau einst zerbricht.
Ihr Dichter, schreibt ! wir wollen's lesen :
Sie ist der Tugend Eigenthum,
Der Unterthanen Lust und Ruhm,
Der Königinnen Preis gewesen.]

Since Bach unquestionably set this libretto to music,
it cannot be doubted that Picander wrote it to accord
with his wishes. Therefore it is interesting to remark
that it makes the minimum call on the composer for
concerted music. It contains even fewer lyrical
stanzas than the St. John Passion, and though St. Mark's
chapters are as rich in incident as St. Matthew's, the
author generally prefers a Choral—of which there are
more than in either the St. John or St. Matthew
Passions—to original reflective material. Moreover,
St. Mark's narrative is remarkable for the comparative
paucity of Choruses founded on the Bible text :
there are only ten (eleven if ' Crucify ' is counted
twice). Assuming that Bach set them as in the
St. Matthew Passion (which contains them all), he
would need to provide no more than ninety bars of
music. The impression which these facts establish is
deepened by the circumstance that even for Picander's
original stanzas Bach used old material. Clearly he

was anxious that the Passion for 1731 should make
the smallest call upon him.   The explanation is
probably found in his circumstances at Leipzig, which
were so unsatisfactory in the late autumn of 1730
that he was even ready to accept an appointment
elsewhere.[1]   If he was composing the Passion required
for 1731 at a moment when he was least disposed to
make considerable effort towards its production, the
character of Picander's libretto is explained.

[1] See his letter in Spitta, ii. 254.

V. *The St. Luke Passion*

BREITKOPF'S Michaelmas 1761 Catalogue printed the following item: 'Bach, J. S., Capellmeisters und Musikdirectors in Leipzig, Passion unsers Herrn Jesu Christi, nach dem Evangelisten Lucas, *à* 2 *Traversi,* 2 *Oboi, Taille, Bassono,* 2 *Violini, Viola,* 5 *Voci ed Organo.*' It was published as genuine by the Bachgesellschaft (Jahrg. XLV (2)) in 1898, and the vocal Score is printed as Bach's by Breitkopf and Härtel. The original Score, formerly belonging to Franz Hauser, is now in the Preuss. Staatsbibliothek (P. 30). It bears the title, but not in Bach's hand, *Passion nach dem Evangelist Lucas von Hr. J. S. Bach in Leipzig.* The libretto, in two Parts, sets forth St. Luke's chapters xxii and xxiii. 1–53. Like the St. Mark Passion, it is almost entirely made up of Bible verses and Hymn stanzas. There are only eight lyrical numbers in it (1 Chorus, 7 Arias), whereas thirty-two of its seventy-nine movements are Chorals. In Part I the alternation of 'Evangelium' and 'Choral' is broken only three times; in Part II only five.

But is the work authentic? Spitta [1] accepted it as genuine, assigning the libretto to 1710, the music to Bach's early Weimar period, and its performance at Leipzig to 1732–4, when the existing Score was written. For his conclusion Spitta relied upon the fact that the manuscript bears Bach's characteristic

[1] ii. 511.

dedication, ' J. J.', and upon the assumption that the manuscript is in his handwriting. In fact it is auto-graph only in part. Of its fifty-seven pages only the first twenty-two and part of the twenty-third were written by Bach ; the remainder are in the hand-writing of his son, C. P. Emanuel.[1] The most con-clusive evidence against the authenticity of the Passion is the music itself. Even Spitta admitted that the dramatic Choruses lack Bach's distinction, while the Recitatives appear to be the work of a composer little practised in writing them. It may be added that the Chorals also afford no evidence of Bach's genius: many of the tunes do not occur elsewhere in his authentic works : and others appear in forms which he nowhere else employed. It was, in fact, upon the evidence of a single Choral, 'Weide mich und mach' mich satt ' (No. 9), that Mendelssohn repudiated Bach's author-ship of the whole work. Writing in 1838 to Franz Hauser, who had purchased the supposed Autograph, Mendelssohn said : 'I am sorry to hear you have given so much money for the St. Luke Passion. No doubt, as an authentic autograph, it would. be worth the price. But it is not by Bach. You ask, " On what grounds do you maintain your opinion ? " I answer, on intrinsic evidence ; though it is unpleasant to have to say so, since it is your property. But just look at the Choral, " Weide mich und mach' mich satt " ! If that is by Sebastian, may I be hanged ! And yet it certainly is in his handwriting. But it is too clean. Evidently he copied it. " Whose is it ? " you ask ; " by Telemann, or M. Bach, or Altnichol ? "[2] Jung Nichol or plain Nichol, how can I tell ? It's not by Bach.' Probably it is of North German origin.

---

[1] Cf. *Bach-Jahrbuch*, 1911, p. 105 f.
[2] Bach's son-in-law.

Conclusion

A CONCLUSION may now be stated. The information in the ' Nekrolog ', repeated by Forkel, is incorrect : Bach composed three, probably four, but not five Passions. Nor was there need for him to write more than we know him to have done. Rost's notes prove that the Passion was sung uninterruptedly and alternately in the two churches from 1723 to 1738, excepting 1733, when public mourning for the King-Elector silenced the Organs. Assuming that the Passion was sung regularly thenceforward till 1750, the year of Bach's death, we have twenty-seven Good Fridays on which Passion music was performed. That Bach sometimes produced the work of other composers has been shown, and reasons can be adduced to conclude that of the twenty-seven Passions performed by him not more than half were his own. Among the ' Acta ' of the Leipzig Council is a document dated 3 April 1724, from which we learn that Bach had endeavoured to break the rule of alternation which allotted the Good Friday performance to St. Nicholas's in that year. His principal reason was the inadequacy of its accommodation for his singers and players. Hence we may conclude that Bach did not perform his own Passions there, an inference supported by ascertained facts : every one of his Passions was produced in St. Thomas's (1723, 1725, 1729, 1731) : the St. John certainly and the St. Matthew most probably had their second performances in that church (1727, 1736).

It may be assumed therefore with some confidence that the call upon Bach to compose or repeat his own Passions was limited to the Good Fridays when St. Thomas's was the appointed church. They fell in 1723, 1725, 1727, 1729, 1731, 1734, 1736, 1738, 1740, 1742, 1744, 1746, 1748, 1750, fourteen in all. To meet this demand he wrote three, probably four, Passions within the first decade of his appointment. If each of these works was sung no more than four times, their number sufficed to fulfil their composer's obligations. The evidence of the Parts suggests that the St. John Passion was performed precisely that number of times. Produced in 1729, the St. Matthew Passion probably was first repeated in 1736 : in other words, two Good Fridays (1731 and 1734) passed at St. Thomas's between the two performances. The first was marked by the production of the St. Mark Passion : the second may have witnessed the third performance of the St. John. Certainly from 1731 onwards the library of the Thomasschule possessed such a number of its Cantor's Passions as, heard in rotation in the principal church over a span of twenty-seven years, could not become so cheapened by excessive use as to call for an addition to that number. Nor, after the St. Matthew Passion was written, could Bach feel he had more to say in that form. The St. Mark Passion of 1731, written after the St. Matthew Passion, stands, as has been shown, in another category.